McKinney Women Making A Difference

McKinney Women
Making
A Difference

A Unique Collection of Stories From Twelve Courageous Women

Dedication

To the Inspiration gained through the reading of these beautiful stories, candidly shared by twelve courageous women who have allowed us a slight glimpse of their life experiences and what drives them.

To the women individually for their strength, hope and guidance and to the many lives they have touched through their charities, scholarships and passions. They bring God's love to life by serving others.

And to my precious husband who continues to fan the flame within my soul!

Foreword

The City of McKinney has received recognition over the past several years for its commitment to quality development, commitment to the preservation of our history and historic charm that McKinney has enjoyed for many years, and our commitment to each other as citizens whether young or old. Each of the women in this book has impacted our city in a positive way by volunteering their time and talents to various organizations for the betterment of our community. William Shakespeare once said "What is a City but the people." I have often said that the greatest assets we have in McKinney are the people who live here and give of themselves to help make McKinney the best place to live in America.

Mayor Brian Loughmiller

A Message from the President...

I am so pleased that Sheila Johnson made it a priority to collect and document the stories of some amazing women in McKinney. Their personal journeys show not only their commitment to their families and their careers but also the contributions they have made to our community.

The McKinney Chamber of Commerce strongly invests in leadership programs such as Leadership McKinney because we know that one of our most important responsibilities is to help create leaders like these women to guide our communities well into the future. As Margaret Mead said, "Never doubt that a small group of thoughtful, committed citizens can change the world; indeed, it's the only thing that ever has."

The impact that these strong women have had on our community will be felt for many years to come. It is a wonderful opportunity to stop and recognize the contributions of those who are the fabric of our community. I look forward to sharing these stories with my own daughters as we continue to develop the next generation of strong female leaders.

Jodi Ann LaFreniere Ray, CCE
President & CEO
McKinney Chamber of Commerce

Introduction

The women in this book need no introduction. They are each known in McKinney for who they are and their special contributions to our community. However, I must let you know that I have been touched by each one of them. So I thought it fitting that in some way a compilation of their stories might serve to recognize them while enlightening, encouraging and inspiring the reader to boldly step up and dare to be a difference maker.

These strong women make a better world for us all. As trail blazers, philanthropists, and community activists, there is no stopping them. They have dreams, visions and goals and their legacies will endure.

I am honored that they agreed to participate in this project and in return this book honors them.

YOU CAN MAKE A DIFFERENCE!

Testimonials

Amanda Baker Adams testimonials -

Amanda brought a unique passion and respect for our armed forces and their families in her tireless work for the USO. Whether with a smile, a hug, a few words of kindness, or an inspirational song, she let each one know how much their sacrifices and service were honored, appreciated and remembered by the American people.

Denny Shupe, Liberty USO President

Amanda truly exhibits what it is to have a pure heart that seeks Godly wisdom and love in every aspect of her life. In the nearly two decades of our close friendship, I've seen her pour her entire heart and soul into her family, friends, arts and music and her beloved community. Amanda loves. And it's that love that enables her to give ALL that she has to those around her without regard for any personal sacrifice. It's character we all can admire and I personally strive to emulate based on her example...

Christa Shaub, CEO,
Shaub Entertainment & Artist
Management Partner,
Primary Wave Music
New York, NY

Erin Botsford testimonials -

I found Erin Botsford to be a model philanthropist on behalf of our ministry to military members and their families. She not only supported the cause with her time, talents, and treasure; but helped others become good stewards in the process. As a result, Erin made a tremendous difference in the lives of military men, women, and families around this entire nation. Her generous and joyful giving was contagious, certainly making her a woman of influence in McKinney, and beyond. I cannot think of a better role model for selfless and effective stewardship than Erin Botsford.

Robert F. Dees, Major General,
U.S. Army, Retired
Former Director, Campus Crusade
Military Ministry

Erin Botsford is an exceptional lady who has inspired me on many occasions. Her wisdom, kindness, strength, candor, generosity and wealth of experience make her an asset to any audience and a joy to learn from. Your life will be richer by learning from hers.

Joel Scrivner, Author/Speaker/Pastor
Covenant Church McKinney

Dr. Jennifer Buchanan testimonial -

Dr. Jennifer Buchanan is an amazing woman. She is full of energy and life. She lives in abundance and always gives more than she gets. She is the most selfless person I know, she is always thinking of others. She is a great visionary, she sees success before it happens. Aside from being a successful orthodontist she has created an amazing charity to help build homes for wounded veterans. This charity has grown an built many homes for deserving men and women who serve our great country. I look up to Jennifer in many aspects, she is truly amazing in what she can accomplish yet she is very humble grateful and thankful. Thank you Jennifer for making our community better and for being a great role model for young girls.

Brittany Lang, LPGA golfer

Dr. Jennifer Buchanan is not your ordinary citizen; she is driven in every aspect to improve the livelihood of our community members and concentrates on serving others.

Jennifer is a master at building strong rapport with her patients, community supporters and military members. She understands the needs of the community and gears her style/approach to creating a "win-win" situation for the individual and for the charitable organization. Her many years of clinical and business acumen serve the community well as she truly understands the model for giving back to those in need.

Jennifer is always focused upon the best quality care for her patients. She works very hard to seek out the very latest technology to promote excellent care. I am honored to know her and support her charitable causes.

Elizabeth R. Tuma
Vice President – Sales
Hospital Corporation of America, Inc.
Beth.Tuma@HCAHealthcare.com

Dr. Jennifer Buchanan is a life changer. Those whose paths cross with hers are truly blessed and better for it. Dr. Buchanan has built a successful orthodontic practice in McKinney, Texas, where she is undeniably passionate about serving her patients. As you can imagine, life-changing leaders do not remain complacent, and Dr. Buchanan's actions reflect this. She also launched Smiles Charity to benefit charitable organizations that build homes for deserving families. This is a person with an incredibly giving heart. She sees no obstacles to achieving goals and making dreams come true for other people. Dr. Buchanan changes lives by giving of her time, her energy, and amazing love for helping others succeed. It's encouraging and reassuring to have such a positive, can-do person in our community.

Vern Herbel
President and CEO
United American Insurance Company

Stephanie Henry testimonials -

Stephanie Henry is a true heart-centered leader. She always puts passion and purpose above profits and in doing so has touched countless lives.

Best, Jeff Crilley
CEO of Real News PR

Stephanie Henry is a courageous woman on a noble mission, driven by a passionate vision and guided by a generous heart.

Pam Wenzel
Author, *Spa Water*

Sheila Johnson testimonials -

Sheila is a dynamic woman who is passionate about helping women become more engaged in their financial lives. She has committed her time and talents to hosting events for women that inspire and promote sound financial planning.

Adri Miller-Heckman President,
Adri Miller Consulting
Author, *Keys to the Ladies Room*

Sheila's tireless commitment to her community and to her clients is an example for us all. Her dedication to making lives better whether through charity work or her financial services practice inspires us all to get involved and serve others selflessly.

Ann M Hughes, Founder and President
of The Female Affect

Knowledge is power. By empowering females with financial education through her study groups, workshops, and working with them individually, Sheila Johnson has changed the lives of many women. She has inspired and enabled these women to take control of their own financial story. She has truly made a difference. I have had the opportunity to see these women grow as a result of Sheila's work, and I am thankful she is there for them.

Robin Spyker, CFP, CIMA
Vice President Prudential Annuities

Angela Paxton testimonials –

What an inspiring true story, especially when you hear…the "rest of the story!" With tears in my eyes, I've not only known it, but have also shared it. Those who know Angela personally admire and respect her profoundly—these pages will let you know why.

June Hunt, Founder, CEO & CSO
(Chief Servant Officer)
Hope for the Heart
Author, *Seeing Yourself
Through God's Eyes*

Angela's story is moving and powerful in that it is a story of three women who were selfless and courageous. Angela has encouraged and helped so many in McKinney and beyond with her love and servant heart. Now we know why…

Texas State Representative
Jodie Laubenberg
Author of House Bill 2, Texas'
Landmark Pro-life Legislation

When you encounter Amanda Baker Adams, you will find an enthusiastic woman filled with life. At First United Methodist of McKinney we have been blessed many times by her singing voice that uplifts and encourages. Although she has been through much in her life, she has emerged a woman of godly joy!

Rev. Douglas Fox
Wellspring Preaching Pastor
First United Methodist Church
of McKinney

Judy Pogue testimonials -

Judy Pogue is a treasure. She fills every room she enters with grace, love and compassion. Her warmth for and acceptance of others regardless of their circumstance is a reflection of her unshakable faith and trust in Jesus

Richard Abernathy, Attorney at Law

Judy [Pogue] is an amazing woman of God who is working to change our nation through prayer and instilling Biblical principles. She has used God's gifts to bring hope and encouragement to the world around her.

Senator Rick Santorum

The Pogue family have been outstanding leaders in our community for many years. Their values, faith, and commitment to family and their community have improved the lives and positively impacted our area, leaving a legacy that continues today.

Judy is a wonderful example of a Godly wife who has dedicated her life in service to God, her family, and to others. She leads by example, living a life that honors the power of prayer and reflects God's love and His grace that He offers to all. She is truly a light of the world that cannot be hidden. [Matthew 5:14]

Congressman Ralph Hall

Michelle Prince testimonials -

Michelle Prince is a powerful business woman, top Zig Ziglar Certified Trainer and the person you want in your corner when writing a book. She will help you "Catch Fire" in your business life and personal life! She's highly motivated to help you succeed personally and professionally. I highly recommend her to all of my chiropractic and doctor clients!

Dr. Chandler George
D.C. CatchFireCoaching.com

Michelle Prince is a PHENOMENAL human being! From the first time I met her at the Zig Ziglar studios, I loved her passion for helping others. She has been a favorite speaker at my conferences, and her writings are very inspirational. You'll be blessed to learn from Michelle Prince!

Howard "Phenomenal" Partridge,
Author of *The 5 Secrets*
of a Phenomenal Business

Keresa Richardson testimonials -

Keresa is known for more than just her business prowess, she is also respected for her commitment to the area via charitable organizations and community involvement. She graciously invests her very valuable time and energy to help others succeed and for the betterment of the community.

Texas State Representative
Scott Sanford

Keresa Richardson is a wonderful example of a successful business woman devoted to her community and family. She is a gracious arts patroness and enthusiast, whose support and interest have been invaluable.

Kevyn Robertson
McKinney Summer Musicals

Wendy Shelley testimonials -

Wendy Shelley is an example of an inspirational leader. She works tirelessly with her church, her children's schools, political awareness in our community, various charitable organizations and events, a women's group doing so with a sense of purpose and conviction for others. She instinctively knows how to delegate and is never one seeking to be singled out for her talents & accomplishments. Wendy Shelley is the true definition of SERVICE LEADERSHIP!

Ray Ricchi
Executive Director of Meals on Wheels,
Collin County and McKinney
City Councilman

Wendy is one those people that inspires people around her, including and especially me. As someone who preaches the value of community engagement, it's refreshing to see someone who values her community and others often over herself. She has a clear love of God, her family and the city of McKinney, and it shows in her schedule. If there were a church full of people like Wendy, there's no limit to the amount of compassionate justice that could be established in our world.

David Lessner Pastor,
Stonebridge Methodist Church

Lynne Sipiora testimonials -

Lynne Sipiora is the consummate professional. Her chosen occupation is not a job but quite obviously a labor of love for which the Samaritan Inn and all those who have the pleasure of interaction with her are the better for it. The community is a better place by virtue of her presence.

Travis Ussery, CPA
McKinney City Council Mayor ProTem

Lynne Sipiora is a woman of action, a wonderful balance of compassion and principle, with a dash of drill sergeant. She influences our entire county every day with her energy and commitment to help our homeless.

> Keith Self, County Judge,
> Collin County, Texas

Maylee Thomas-Fuller testimonials -

Maylee has never passed up an opportunity to serve those in need. More impressive though, Maylee never waits for that opportunity to present itself...she seeks it out, again and again!

> George Fuller Chairman,
> McKinney Community Development
> Company

Maylee Thomas-Fuller is a dedicated and truly passionate advocate for children. Her strong and beautiful voice has inspired many to follow her lead in helping at-risk and disadvantaged children to again love life.

> Carol Schaue, Senior Gift Officer
> Legacy Children's Medical
> Center Foundation

Maylee Thomas-Fuller is a shining star in McKinney. Her positive impact and generosity in our community is truly inspiring. The world is a better place because she is in it!

> Rick Wells
> Wells Hospitality Group

Table of Contents

Lions and Elephants and Sharks, Oh My!

By Amanda Baker Adams

Elephant in the Room:

- A metaphorical idiom for an obvious truth
or issue that is being ignored.

I've spent weeks trying to write this amazing inspirational piece on how to make a difference in the community. As I sit here now, the night before the deadline to turn in this "life changing" piece, I have erased everything I had written, and I am praying for a miracle. What could I possibly say that is interesting much less inspirational at this point?

I am currently a sleep deprived mother to an eight week old who has been using my clothes and hair as his personal spit up cloth, and to a kindergartener who doesn't understand why her mother hasn't taken a shower in a week. I am a wife to a very understanding husband who hasn't made fun of the fact that our dinners have consisted of whatever you can find in the kitchen that doesn't look like it could be used for a science fair project. I am the daughter to amazing parents who continue to support and love me even when I ask for their help to watch the kids as I'm pulling into their driveway. I am a big sister to an incredibly smart, funny, and beautiful little sister who doesn't care that I forgot her birthday this year. And, I am the CEO of a company that was just brutally attacked by "sharks" in front of six million viewers on ABC's hit show, *Shark Tank*. Why would anyone want to listen to what I have to say? You might not, but that's okay, because I am also a princess to a heavenly King who loves me unconditionally and can use me to make a difference just the way I am right now…smelly, sleep deprived, imperfect, selfish, forgetful, and humbled. I don't know if my story is very interesting or inspiring, but it is the one God has blessed me with and I pray that you can learn something from it.

I grew up in McKinney, Texas. My family moved here from Colorado when I was nine. In the mid 80's, McKinney basically had a Dairy Queen and the town completely shut down on Friday nights to watch the Lions play football. I thought that my life was over. My father was starting his State Farm Insurance business in the historic downtown square when it looked like a ghost town due to the recession. My family was also struggling financially, and if it wasn't for the kindness of neighbors who took a chance on complete strangers, we probably would not be here today. People looked out for others and took pride in their Texas small town even before McKinney was the second best place to live in America.

My parents taught me what it meant to make a difference in the community. Although my dad was extremely busy starting a new business, he always put his family first. He was on the school board, involved with several service groups, very active in our church, and somehow never missed an activity that my sister and I were busy doing. My mother was the backbone of our family, and I am just starting to realize all of the sacrifices that she made being our taxi driver, nurse, tailor, chef, maid, and counselor. My parents raised me to love the Lord, respect my elders, and to follow my dreams. When I graduated from high school, I had no idea what I wanted to do, but I knew that I wanted to make a difference. My dreams took me to college in Nashville to be a Christian singer. Belmont University helped me to become a strong performer. I ended up with opportunities which took me around the world singing and dancing. I eventually landed in New York City for some of the best experiences of my life. While I was busy working on my career, my dreams of making a difference in the world began to slowly fade into the brightness of the New York City lights. Little did I know how an event that changed the city's skyline would also forever change my life.

In 2001, I was singing for the USO, a civilian run service organization started by Bob Hope in 1941 supporting the troops and veterans at home and abroad. We were sent down to Ground Zero a few days after the Twin Towers were reduced to a mountain of ash. Our mission was to raise spirits and help bring relief to the middle of hell on earth. I was singing the favorite songs of the workers searching through the rubble for loved ones, listening to their stories of missing relatives and friends, while somehow experiencing little miracles of hope. People from every walk of life were uniting…laughing, crying, sharing, and bonding through one of the worst tragedies in American history. But then people began to forget. The rest of the world could turn off the TV when it became too painful to watch, but I and the rest of New York was still living in hell. I didn't realize the effects that 9/11 had on me until I was diagnosed with post traumatic stress disorder seven years later. During these dark years I was still singing in bands, doing Broadway shows, having worldly success, going to church, but nothing seemed important anymore. Everything seemed meaningless…I had become numb. In my depression, I started making careless choices. Instead of pressing into God for direction and guidance, I let my apathy choose my path which eventually led me home.

I had left McKinney a superlative queen…Miss McKinney High

School, head cheerleader, president of the student body, my youth group, choir, blah, blah, blah…and came back a prodigal daughter with a scarlet letter on my chest. I was pregnant, jobless, ashamed, and completely defeated. Making a difference was definitely the last item on my to do list. Since my plans were not turning out like I wanted, maybe it was time

Singing at the Susan G. Komen Race for the Cure, Dallas, Texas

to start listening to what God might have planned for me instead. Luckily, my God is a God of mercy, forgiveness, grace, and love. He restored my life, gave me hope, and another chance. Only God could have planned the next chapter of my life.

The same year I came home, my future husband, Jason, moved from California to McKinney to be with his daughter. It took four years of God preparing our hearts to finally introduce us to each other through the queen of McKinney Women Making a Difference, Judy Pogue. After a ten minute meeting at Starbucks, we knew we had found something unique and real. I had told my mother, after our first date, that I had met the man I was going to marry, and came to find out that he had told his friend the same thing.

Two weeks into dating, Jason showed up at one of my gigs with a large stuffed elephant. I asked him, "What's the elephant in the room?" He wanted to start a conversation about getting married and didn't know

how to bring it up, so he used the elephant to break the ice. I thought it was cute and creative. Our conversation went very well, because a few weeks later we were married. His use of "the elephant in the room" sparked an idea that soon became our company, Elephant Chat.

The harsh realities of blending a family began immediately. We had thirty something years of baggage we were bringing into our relationship which meant there were going to be several more "elephants" to be discussed. With the divorce rate in America being over fifty percent for first marriages and over sixty percent for second marriages, we did not want to become another statistic. We tried to tackle these "elephants" head on, but had so much anxiety around how to bring up the topics that we hardly ever got to discus the real issues. We needed a light hearted and loving way to bring up these "we need to talk" conversations, so out came the stuffed elephant. We started calling our tough conversations "elephant chats". As we began to share with friends our approach to communication, we noticed that our friends began to open up and share the struggles that they were going through. As people stopped ignoring their own elephants, some amazing changes began to happen in their relationships. People loved this "elephant" concept so much that we were able to raise enough seed capital to see if we could turn this funny idea into an actual product that could help others.

We've always known God was in the middle of this venture because relationships began to form and contacts were made in a way that only God could orchestrate. From designers to manufacturers, and engineers to marriage counselors, Elephant Chat began to take shape based on the product principles that Jason and I had come up with: indestructible, fragile, patient, and significant.

We designed a cube shaped art piece that sits out as a constant reminder of the importance of good communication. When there is an issue to be discussed, the cube is removed to reveal an elephant stuffed

Elephant Chat Mascot

uncomfortably in a clear casing. It can be used as a non-verbal reminder for smaller issues like placing it on the toilet seat that has been left up one too many times. The elephant can also be taken out to be used as a "referee" between the two people having the conversation. Whoever is holding the elephant has permission to talk and so that the conversation doesn't become one sided, we included a timer for both parties to get the chance to be heard.

While we were in the middle of creating this communication tool to help restore relationships, the stresses in our own life were beginning to take their toll on our own relationship. I found out that I was pregnant with a boy to add to our beautiful blended family. While Jason and I struggled to communicate about our multiplying elephants, the opportunity to be on *Shark Tank* appeared. The producers loved our little elephant prototype and the next few months were filled with extensive background checks, mounds of legal paper work, and honing our pitch. Out of forty thousand hopeful entrepreneurs, we were finally invited to Los Angeles to meet the "sharks" and tape our episode. Jason and I spent countless late night hours working on Elephant Chat. The knowledge that we gained from speaking to several marriage counselors and researching the best communication methods, not only strengthened our product, but also our marriage. With the added help of several prayer warriors, our marriage wasn't just surviving anymore, but it was beginning to finally thrive.

Eight and half months pregnant, we were ready to dive into the deep end with the sharks. After an hour long swim, we left the tank excited and hopeful for the future of Elephant Chat. The sharks loved the concept and had several positive suggestions and comments. A few weeks later, a production team arrived in McKinney to tape our family and get a better behind the scenes look at our product. You can imagine our surprise and devastation when we watched our episode after an extensive hatchet job of editing. Our exciting and positive swim had been turned into a brutal shark attack that we barely survived. However we did survive, lived to tell the tale, and our relationship and company is better for it. We have given control over to God and know that He can use Elephant Chat to make a difference in relationships if that is His plan.

I don't know if any of the 2,000 word summary of my life has inspired you or given you ideas on how you can make a difference in your community. However, I hope that you can at least take away one thing…God's love for you. No matter where you are in your life, God can meet you there, give you hope, and restore your soul as He did mine. As women we put so much pressure on ourselves to be everything to everyone…to look perfect, act perfect, and be perfect. We feel like we can't make a difference unless we're super mom, president of every committee, work full time, run a non-profit, and still have dinner on the table by five. These are lies and stresses we have put on ourselves that only hinder us from being who we're meant to be. As long as we are listening to who God has called us to be and what He has called us to do, we will not only make a difference in McKinney, but we can help change the world. Right now God has called me to feed my screaming hungry baby. Blessings to you all!

Update - The day after I turned in my article for editing, NBC's the *Today Show* called and featured Elephant Chat with Kathie Lee and Hoda. They loved the product, and we've received lots of positive feedback and sales from all over the country. Favor of God. ☞

AMANDA BAKER ADAMS

Amanda Baker Adams' singing career began in the church at age three. After a three decade journey of professional and personal successes and struggles, she has come home to her Texas roots humbled and amazed by God's faithfulness, mercy, and grace. Leading worship in churches around the Dallas/Fort Worth Metroplex, and the CEO of a conflict resolution company she started with her husband, Elephant Chat Inc., she is finally listening to God's plan instead of her own while witnessing God redeem and transform hearts and lives

Amanda Baker Adams spent the last eighteen years performing in several New York, Nashville, and Dallas based bands, Broadway shows, international tours, and concerts including Grease, Footloose, the Musical, *and the* USO. *While performing with the United Service Organizations of Metropolitan New York, she had the privilege to travel internationally entertaining active military, veterans, and numerous celebrity and political figures, including the President of the United States.*

Other career highlights include: Appearance on Sean Hannity's national radio program; The Inaugural Rock and Country Band for Disney's Premiere Ship, Disney Magic; *performing at the* Grand Ole Opry; *appearances in television and film; and numerous roles in musical theatre (AEA). Amanda Baker Adams graduated with honors from Belmont University in Nashville, TN. Her original music and more information is available at www.elephantchat.com and www.amandabaker.com*

Elephant Chat Inc.

1.855.ELE.CHAT

The Gift of Giving

By Erin Botsford, CEO, President, The Botsford Group
Author of *The Big Retirement Risk:*
Running Out of Money Before You Run Out of Time

My husband and I have a silly rule we have tried to live by: We try to be anonymous in our giving. We always say: "If anyone knows we gave a gift, it doesn't count." I know that may sound silly and it probably is, but we have never tried to draw attention to ourselves through our giving. This makes writing this chapter or being included in this book particularly difficult. That being said, if my life, my struggles to get out of poverty, my work or my giving can inspire someone else, I guess it's worth violating our rule. After all, it was self-imposed.

My story is a wonderful one, wrought with twists and turns and a lot of opportunities for personal growth and development. I was raised in a loving home, the fifth of six children in a small town south of Chicago. My father was a teacher, a professor at Northwestern University at one point in time. When I was eleven, he decided to pursue his dream to open a clinic for early childhood education in San Diego, California, a place he had visited during the war. He borrowed against his teacher's pension plan, wrote a book, and we moved to San Diego. Six months after we moved to California, my father died of a massive heart attack at home, in front of all six children. He was only fifty.

Life immediately changed for our family. Dad only had a $10,000 life insurance policy. Because he had borrowed from his teacher's pension plan, there was no pension benefit available. We all had to go to work to put food on the table and to keep a roof over our heads. I babysat, raked leaves and did whatever I could to contribute, as did all of my siblings. None of us regrets that; we all developed a good work ethic as a result.

Unfortunately, we were barely scraping by when tragedy struck again. I was sixteen, driving to my first "real" job at McDonald's, when I was involved in a terrible accident with a motorcyclist. The driver of the motorcycle was killed, and I was charged with involuntary manslaughter by the State of California. My mother and I met with an attorney and were honest about our family's financial situation. After hearing our story, he spoke to my mother as if I were not there. "Mrs. McGowan," he said, "this is purely a matter of economics. If your daughter will plead guilty to these charges, I will be happy to enter the plea at no cost to you. As a result, your daughter will get the appropriate sentence prescribed by the State of California. However, if she wants to defend herself it will cost you a lot of money."

Since we had no money, my mother instantly realized that our choices were limited. She thanked the attorney and agreed that I had no option other than to plead guilty. To say that I was horrified would be an understatement. I begged and pleaded with my mother. That's when she looked at me and said the ten words I will never forget, "Honey, we have no money; therefore, we have no choice." That was the day I learned that money can buy you choices. Fortunately, the case wasn't closed. My older brother had just begun his real estate career; he suggested that we take a second mortgage on our home to pay for my defense. With the money from the mortgage, our attorney was able to bring in expert witnesses who proved that the motorcyclist was driving well over the speed limit, and that he had hit me, not the other way around. The judge dropped the charges. At the end of the court proceeding, he said, "Take this little girl home; she's been through enough."

I wish the story had ended there, but it didn't. Shortly after the criminal proceeding, the family of the motorcyclist sued my mother and me for a substantial sum of money. My mother was terrified that we would lose the only asset that she possessed, our family home. At one point, in her most fearful moment, my mother looked at me and said: "Well, because of YOU, we may have to pitch a tent on the high school football field!" Words are powerful; I can't describe the impact that those words left on me. Fortunately, her fears were not realized; the case was finally settled at the eleventh hour by our auto insurance company.

The interesting part of this entire tragedy was that this experience formed the entire basis for the business I have now owned for over twenty-five years. I didn't know it at the time, but I can now look back and see that God was teaching me really valuable lessons about things like risk management and asset protection, which I use every day to help clients avoid the risk of losing everything they have worked for.

Continuing my story, through my diligent savings and a fortuitous winning appearance on the *Wheel of Fortune* (ironically solving the puzzle "Down in the Dumps"), I accumulated a nest egg of about $22,000, which was no small sum in 1979. Shortly before I married, I invested $3,000 to buy a townhouse in San Diego County with a friend. This investment worked out well. However, soon after we married, my husband, Bob and I entrusted the balance of our savings to a stockbroker, who lost all of it in a very short period of time. I was devastated. While it may not have been much money to our broker, it was everything to us, and it represented years of hard work and sacrifice. From that day forward, I made it my personal mission to learn everything that I could about money and investing. I was determined never to let what happened to us happen to anyone I cared about. It was this tragic experience, I believe, that helped me to become one of the top Financial Advisors in the entire country. I am ranked among the top 100! Where would I be today without these valuable personal lessons?

My story did get better—I married my high school sweetheart, who became a fighter pilot in the U.S. Air Force and ended up as an airline pilot. We moved seventeen times in the first fourteen years that we were married, all of which I considered to be great adventures. Another benefit to those moves was that each time we moved, I was able to 'reinvent' myself. When I left my small town, I was a beaten down, very emotionally damaged young girl. In my town, I was always known as "the girl that killed that boy." Once I left that place, I never let anyone know about the car accident. I wanted to forget that part of my life. I didn't realize it was that part of my life that made me the person that I am today.

Our life of giving and making a difference came gradually. After all, being raised in poverty and then marrying a military man isn't normally the formula for having extra resources to give. But at the age of thirty, I began my financial planning practice and it was blessed. By the age of forty, I was making a substantial amount of money and my desire to give back grew more and more. There is an age-old saying I believe with all my heart: "You can't out give God!" I give God all of the credit for being my partner in business. He alone deserves all of the credit and glory for any financial success that I have enjoyed. I decided to partner with God and help those less fortunate than me. I wanted to do it anonymously, if at all possible. My thought was this: there are people out there who are struggling with all kinds of issues. Often, it is in a person's lowest moment that they are apt to get on their knees and pray for God's help. I wanted to be the tool God used to answer their prayers. But I wanted them to see it as coming from God—I was just the conduit. I wanted God to get the thanks and God to get the glory, not me. I contacted the pastor of our church, where I knew they had a "love fund." I told him to let me know if there were specific needs that could be met by writing a check. He would contact me, let me know of the need and then he would arrange to have a check or cash delivered to the person on an anonymous basis. It was so much fun! Sometimes he would report back to me how my check changed that person's life how it strengthened their belief in the power of prayer and how it was just the thing they needed to get their lives back together.

At some point, my husband and I talked to the pastor and told him, while we felt good about the lives we had changed by writing checks, we now needed to step up to the plate and give what was more valuable—our time. Because we both travelled weekly for our work and were gone most weekends, we couldn't be relied upon for a steady time commitment, so we asked him to contact us if there was ever a one-time project that was needed to help someone. A few weeks later, the pastor called asking for some practical help for a couple from the country of Nepal. As it turns out, this couple had received the "diversity visa"—which is basically akin to winning the lottery in third world countries. It is a free pass to come to the United States, given to 1,000 people each year in the poorest of poor nations. This couple had made their way to McKinney, Texas and some-how landed in our church on a Sunday morning. The pastor said these people needed some help learning the driver's handbook so they could sit for the driving test. Clearly, I thought that Bob and I were capable of help-ing with this limited assignment so we met them at a restaurant with the driver's handbook in tow. We didn't know then how involved we would become in their lives, nor what great lessons they would teach us along the way.

It should have been clear from our very first meeting this was going to be a little more work than we had initially anticipated. These people knew very little English, had never driven a car and in fact, had never driven on a paved highway. They were living in a one bedroom apartment next to our church and when we visited with them the first time, there was NOTHING in their apartment except a lone mattress in the bedroom, a few odd dishes and a couple of pieces of silverware. We found out that they both worked the night shift at the local Walmart and walked to and from work each night (about ½ mile each way). We also found out that they didn't know some very basic things. For instance, when they would walk home in the morning, they would stand outside the gate to the apartment, waiting for a car to come out because they didn't know that there was a code on the keypad to open the gate. Sometimes they would stand out there for an hour because they arrived home at 7 am before people were leaving for work. We quickly helped them learn the key code and bought them two "clickers" that would automatically open the gate. Wow, they thought, "what freedom!" To be able to come and go with the press of a clicker!

We did help them with learning the driver's handbook and helped them by paying for driving lessons from the local McKinney driving school. We then realized that they needed a car. They insisted they would NOT accept any gifts from us so we made them a loan and our friend, a leasing agent, helped find them a used car for $4,000. We told them that they could pay us back $100 a month until it was paid off. Knowing they were working for minimum wage on the night shift, we assumed it would take them four years or more to pay us back. Instead, they had the entire loan paid off in 10 months. That seemed amazing to us, considering we found out they were also sending $500 a month back to Nepal to help pay for the care of their two children. Because of a fluke in the immigration system, they had left their children with family members until they could send for them.

Seeing the sparse conditions within their apartment, and considering their stubborn nature to not accept any gifts, we did manage to fool them and told them that when new people arrive in the United States it is an American tradition that they are given a "shower." We told them the host family takes them to a place like Walmart and buys them everything they need to get started in this country. They had trouble believing that Americans would do this for perfect strangers but I guess we were pretty convincing because the next thing I knew we were walking the aisles of Walmart, (with their employee discounts) buying them everything from silverware to dishes to sheets, pots, pans etc. It was so much fun. Helping them set up their apartment and seeing their overwhelming gratitude was nothing short of intoxicating. Finally, they had jobs, a car, an apartment and stuff in the apartment. In their minds, what else would anyone want or need?

For several years, Bob went over to their apartment every Thursday and helped them read through their mail, teaching them what to pay attention to and what to throw out. They had no concept of "junk mail." They thought if someone paid postage to get a package to them, then clearly it was important. We helped them fill out their benefits packages from Walmart, took them to doctor's appointments and helped them in situations where they needed an interpreter.

Paying it forward: At one point, they told us a family member had also received the diversity visa and was now living with them. It was actually a husband, wife and child and they wanted us to come meet them. The five of them had been living in the same one bedroom apartment. Bob and I went over to meet them and they were just as gracious and green as this couple had been. They had such amazing dreams for their future in America. They told us about the struggles in Nepal…that electricity had been reduced to only having power eight hours a day, that the terrorist regimes had taken over and how difficult life had become in that country. To win the diversity visa to them was like any of us winning the

Publisher's Clearing House prize. They were so happy to be here. Both of them had also been hired at Walmart, and had already signed a lease on their new one bedroom apartment. Even though both of them had college educations, they were grateful for their new jobs at Walmart and all of the opportunities that lie ahead.

Our original friend asked if we would loan his niece and her husband the same $4,000 we had lent to them to buy a car. He added he would guarantee payment. Of course, we said "yes." At some point in our conversation, I said:" it must be time to give these people a good old American "shower." How about if we go down to Walmart after church tomorrow and buy them everything they will need to get started? Our friend looked at me, as if in horror. He said: "NO, WE will give them their shower. You did this for us and now we will do it for them, for that is the American Way!" And they did….How about that for paying it forward? This story has such a happy ending. Both couples have subsequently saved enough money to buy homes and are now American citizens.

A final story I thought I would share is about the work we are doing today in Africa. It is a much larger story but the ending is still unknown. My husband and I were fortunate to take several trips to southern Africa, where we were exposed to the abject poverty and the huge need for basic essentials like clean water. A total of 27,000 people die every single day because of the lack of clean water. That statistic alone is a horror to me. In 1999, we started giving substantial sums to fund water wells and orphan homes. In 2010, we were approached with an idea to create/fund a Facebook game, with the idea of leveraging our dollars to fund humanitarian projects in Africa. When we found out the game 'Farmville' made $260 million in its first year and that there was $12 billion being made on social games annually, we decided to step up to the plate and write a very large check to fund our game, "Safari Challenge." We are hoping and praying this effort will create an entire family of social games with the stated objective of "Gaming is Giving™." Our game went live in June, 2013, so the outcome is yet unknown. Suffice it to say we stepped out in faith, since "To whom much is given, much is required…" (*Luke 12:48*)

In conclusion, I would like to encourage anyone who reads this to step out in faith and help just one person. It becomes addictive and the reward of giving is so much greater and larger than I would have ever imagined. We started very small but I believe with all of my heart that God honored our giving and has now entrusted us with larger resources because He knew we would be good stewards of what He has given to us. In the end, it's all His anyway…we just take care of what He has given us for a little while. In the bigger picture, the only reward I want to hear are the words: "Well done, good and faithful servant." Those words and those words alone are the only thing that will count in eternity. ✎

ERIN BOTSFORD

Erin Botsford is the founder and CEO of The Botsford Group, a boutique financial planning firm with offices in Frisco, Texas and Atlanta, Georgia.

Erin's firm specializes in retirement and asset protection planning for business owners and senior executives of Fortune 500 companies. Having trademarked an investment philosophy called "Lifestyle Driven Investing™, she is considered a thought leader on 21st Century investing, risk management and retirement. Among the top echelon of financial advisors, she is often asked to share her views on investing and the economy in keynote addresses across the country. A frequent speaker at industry conferences, Erin has recently published her first book: The Big Retirement Risk: Running out of Money Before You Run out of Time.

Erin's personal story of overcoming poverty and adversity in her early life to becoming one of the Top Financial Planners in the country has been featured in numerous articles and publications. Her business success has been recognized by publications such as Barron's *magazine,* D Magazine, Success Magazine, Investment News, *along with television appearances on* CNBC, Fox News and Bloomberg Television.

Erin Botsford
Erin T. Botsford, CFP®, CRPC
Founder, CEO
The Botsford Group
www.botsfordfinancial.com
ebotsford@botsfordfinancial.com

A Smile Makes a Difference

By Dr. Jennifer Buchanan

*I*t has always been my goal to inspire and make a difference in the lives of others. When I was 10 years old, I was being pushed in a wagon and fell face first into the pavement I chipped my front tooth in half and was devastated! I thought I would never smile again. I lost my self-confidence. Since the chip was so large, the dentist had to put a piece of wire to hold the fake portion of the tooth (luckily technology has improved). I was always self-conscious of it. When I was 12 years old I had orthodontic treatment and it changed my life. After orthodontics I was confident and proud of my smile. It inspired me to pursue a career in orthodontics to help others smile and increase their self-esteem.

A devastating event became a defining moment in my life. I truly believe that you can find the silver lining in any situation. Looking for the positive and having the patience for it to reveal itself is a key to happiness and success. Smiling in the face of adversity is critical. Many friends ask me why I am always in a good mood. I believe that looking for what is right in any situation helps to maintain a positive outlook. I know that God has a purpose for everything in our lives, good and bad. During difficult situations I ask myself, "What am I to learn through this?"

To become an orthodontist, it takes 11 years of school after high school. Through high school I developed good study habits and was able to graduate third in my high school class of 628. When I attended the University of Texas at Austin, all of my classmates were at the top of their high school classes. It became more difficult to be at the top of the class. Austin is also a fun city with many distractions, so it took an extra effort to be focused on academics. I never gave up my goal to be an orthodontist.

One of my most complex courses was Organic Chemistry. I failed the class and became discouraged. However, I did not give up my dream. Instead, I retook the class in summer school. Many people would give up their dream and say to themselves that maybe I am not meant to be an orthodontist. It is too difficult. You have to turn the channel of negative thinking and focus on your dream. You need positive self-talk such as, "I am meant to help others and this has always been my goal. I can do it and will stay strong." This is where the battle is won and lost. Fortunately, my family was very supportive and kept encouraging me to pursue my dream of becoming an orthodontist. Henry Ford said it best, "Whether you think you can or can't, you are right! "Your beliefs drive you and become a self-fulfilling prophecy. "

There are three dental schools in Texas—UT San Antonio, UT Houston, and Baylor. I grew up in San Antonio and would study at the medical library that was adjacent to the Dental School. I always saw myself as attending dental school in San Antonio. I was accepted to Baylor College of Dentistry in Dallas and then to UT Houston. At the time, UT San Antonio did not offer a residency in orthodontics. Both Baylor and UT Houston did have an orthodontic residency. I realized that it was a blessing and that God was leading me in a different direction. I chose Baylor in Dallas. It was such a great decision! Throughout dental school there were many challenges. It was difficult, but I did not give up my vision of becoming an orthodontist.

When I applied to Orthodontic Residency there were 50 programs in the United States and Canada. Most programs take only five students per year. I decided to apply to them all since I wanted to be an orthodontist first and foremost. There was not a match program where you fill out one application that goes to all schools. Instead I had to fill out 50 separate applications using a typewriter! It took me the whole summer since I do not type!

I was first accepted to the orthodontics residency program in Detroit. I was getting set to attend there when the Baylor Orthodontics Program offered me a position. What a blessing! I wanted to stay in Dallas and Baylor was my #1 choice. My instructors were all world class and encouraged me to be my best.

As part of our orthodontics program at Baylor, we did a master's thesis research project. My thesis was "The Psychosocial Impact of Orthodontic Treatment". Recently one of my mentors at Baylor called me and wanted a copy of my thesis since there are students in the orthodontics program that want to continue my research. My thesis found that orthodontic treatment improves the psychosocial functioning and self-concept of patients, leading to a better quality of life. Most of the significant psychosocial changes occur at the end of treatment because patients feel a sense of accomplishment, pride and relief after mastering the challenge of wearing braces.

My mother and father both inspired me to start my own orthodontics practice. My Mom was one of the first saleswomen if not the very first woman to sell copiers for the SCM Corporation. She always made Presidents Club for being top in sales. She then became one of the first women to sell cars. After learning the car business, she opened her own import car dealership. She would travel to Europe to bring back Ferraris, Porsches, and Jaguars, covert them to USA EPA standards and then sell them at a discounted price. She was the only female car dealer at that time. It was amazing to see her pave the way on her own! I learned from her that I could accomplish anything that I put my mind to do.

My father served in the Army where he did his residency to become a pathologist. He had his own M.D. practice with several other pathologists in San Antonio, Texas. I enjoyed going to work with him and seeing the brain and heart specimens. After 20 years in practice, he decided to go back to school to become a board certified dermatologist and dermato-pathologist. He was an incredible "study buddy" and kept me encouraged and motivated when I was struggling.

My father opened three dermatology offices outside of Fort Worth and to help me get started, he opened a satellite office in McKinney. The finish out and lease of the space was done so I would be ready to open the first day after graduation. We would work on Saturdays while I was finishing up my residency. I was his receptionist and nurse assistant. It was a great way to meet patients and "hit the ground running". He taught me about the business of medicine, running an office, paying taxes, payroll, hiring staff, etc. I am so blessed to have his guidance and influence!

Dr. Buchanan pictured with some of her high school patients.

In 1996, I graduated from Baylor and opened my orthodontics practice in McKinney. At that time, McKinney was a small town with a population of 30,000 people (the population now is 130,000+). The people of McKinney and the surrounding areas have been very kind to me.

The Byers Family (2013 Smiles Charity home recipients) with Dr. Buchanan and her husband, Mike Bushanan.

My practice is unique in that we have close relationships with our patients and their families. We share their joys and hardships. Our patients forever become part of our lives. Our office feels like a big extended family. Just as I have watched McKinney grow, I have seen my patients grow and be successful. In 2002, the Chamber of Commerce chose us as the Small Business of the Year. It was a wonderful surprise and honor!

It has been such a blessing to work with my patients and their families. A smile is everything! It is the first thing that people notice about you. A smile is for a lifetime. You may have many cars or live in many houses but you only have one smile. A smile can open doors to success and inspire confidence to pursue dreams. One of my patients moved me to tears when he told me, "Dr. Buchanan, I just want to tell you that you have changed my life forever!"

Orthodontics has typically been thought of as for teenagers and children, but many parents see their children's incredible smiles and seek treatment. It has been so much fun because some of my first patients are now bringing in their children for treatment. I love the circle of orthodontic life!

In my office we also offer orthodontic scholarships for individuals in need. A note I received from one of those patients reaffirmed how important a smile is. She stated, "Hello Dr. Buchanan, I am an old patient of yours from about four-five years ago. You were on my mind today and I just wanted to thank you for everything you did for my family and me by providing braces for me. To this day, I still have people tell me that I have a million dollar smile, and it is all thanks to you."

Since 1998, our office has been working with the Head Start early childhood program to teach dental health. My office visits each classroom of children twice. At the first visit, we show proper brushing habits and health tips. On the second visit, we award Beanie Babies with braces to the children who are demonstrating good dental habits. I have an incredible staff in my office who spend hours placing braces on the 100+ Beanie Babies. Many of my patients and the community have donated the Beanie Babies too!

Our office has been active in supporting Scotty's gifts to donate toys to local children in need since 1999. One of my patients lost a son and started Scotty's gifts in his honor. The holidays are a difficult time for many, so they chose to spread joy and love by having Santa lead a caravan of cars loaded with gifts to donate. My patients and the community have been extremely generous with their donations of toys.

In 2001, the McKinney Rotary Club introduced me to the Lost Boys of Sudan. These boys were three-seven years old when the Taliban killed their parents and they had to wander around Africa to find food and water. Many died from starvation and from lion and alligator attacks.

The Lost Boys had a tradition that was a sign of manhood to extract all of the lower six front teeth. When they were rescued and brought to the United States, they felt self-conscious about their smile as a result of not having their front teeth. Loss of these teeth affected their speech since these teeth are critical for enunciation. Additionally, it caused a tongue thrust to develop that flared the upper teeth into a severe overbite. After hearing their story at Rotary Club, I wanted to do whatever I could to help these courageous boys. My dental colleagues and I partnered together to restore their smiles. It was such a blessing to work with my dental colleagues in McKinney who dedicated their time and talents to restore the Lost Boys' wonderful smiles! The Lost Boys are the most grateful and courteous individuals. They truly demonstrate how adversity makes you stronger!

My goal as an orthodontist is to create functional and attractive smiles for my patients. I also feel that it is important to find ways to inspire them to get active in the community. We began by hosting a skating party with a $5.00 admission that went to build homes for local families in need. I invited my dental colleagues and their patients to participate as well. We were able to donate $5,000-10,000 each year to go towards a home for deserving local families. It has been a joy to work together with my patients and dental colleagues to give back to the community! Our dream became to raise enough funds for an entire home.

When I moved my office to the Adriatica development in McKinney we found the perfect opportunity to reach our goal of building a complete home for a family. Behind my office is an open area flood plain that can hold 20,000 people. It provided an opportunity to give back to the community and to raise more funds to help build homes for those in our area that were in need In 2008, we decided to host a free family outdoor concert to raise funds to build a home. The night before, my husband and I looked over the field and wondered if anyone would attend. Country star Chris Cagle was our headliner and 6,000 fans attended! We were able to host

Crowd shot from behind the stage at the Smiles Charity Concert (Dr. Buchanan's office at top of photo).

a free concert for the community and raised enough money to build an entire home for a deserving family!

In 2009, I was chosen as the McKinney Citizen of the Year. It was such an honor that would have not been possible without the support of my husband, daughter, parents, patients, friends, and the community. Words cannot express the gratitude I feel for their encouragement and love.

One of my very first patients had a dream to serve in the military, especially after he witnessed the atrocities of 9/11. He was killed in action in Afghanistan in 2010 and it strengthened my resolve to do more for those brave men and women who sacrifice everything so that we can be free. Therefore, in 2011, we started working with charities to build homes for our wounded military heroes. We always hold the Smiles Charity concert over Memorial Day Weekend. It was a perfect fit since we wanted to do more for our veterans.

2013 was our best event so far! We had R5, the Maylee Thomas Band, and Ryan Star as our performers. We had a crowd of 12,000 and surpassed our fundraising totals! A wounded military hero and his family will now have a home to call their own!

Our patient skating party became a 501c3 charity called Smiles Charity to build homes for deserving families while providing a free city wide family event. From 2008 to 2013, Smiles Charity has helped build eight homes and has hosted six concerts. It has been amazing having the local community, my patients, friends, family, volunteers, and corporate sponsors to come together to support us! The Smiles Charity committee is 100% volunteer. My friends spend countless hours of their precious time to make Smiles Charity a success. I am so grateful for their dedication! My husband and daughter spend many hours volunteering too! I appreciate their patience with me being busy and taking time away from our family time. My dental colleagues and local businesses have been incredible in supporting Smiles Charity!

You do not have to do big things to make a difference. A smile, small gesture or kind word has power. There is always an opportunity to help and encourage. The key is to take action.

I will conclude with these thoughts that have sustained me. Smile through adversity, have a spirit of gratitude. Maintain persistence and take action. Stay positive and be patient. Do not give up on your dreams. With prayers ask, believe, and you shall receive. Remember, serving others is the highest calling and greatest blessing. ⚯

DR. JENNIFER BUCHAHNAN

Dr. Jennifer Buchanan opened her orthodontic practice in 1996. Her goal is to increase the self-esteem of her patients while encouraging community service. She has won numerous awards including: Readers Choice Best Ortho- dontist 2008-2013, Small Business of the Year 2002, McKinney Citizen of the Year 2009, HGTV Community Crusader 2010, and Texas Monthly Super Dentist 2006-2012. She founded Smiles Charity in 2008 and resides in McKinney, TX with her husband and daughter. For more information please go to www.mckinneybrac- es.com and www.smilescharity.org.

Dr. Jennifer Buchanan, Orthodontist
6595 Virginia Parkway, Suite 100
McKinney, Texas 75071
972-542-4412
jennifer_buchanan@sbcglobal.net

———❖———

Zoe's Children

By Stephanie Henry

Curled up in an uncomfortable position on a hard couch, waiting out a six-hour layover in London after an eight-hour flight from Nairobi, I was trying to sleep. Mary had puffed up her new Kenya bag, making a makeshift pillow for me.

"Mom," she said, smiling, "I can't believe we really went to Africa."

"I know, baby, we did, and it will change us forever."

Our trip to Kenya was part of a mission called Zoe Ministry. We met our group of twelve in London en route to Kenya, and now we were all departing from one another to head home to our different states. I've continued to find fulfillment through giving, listening, and acts of service. Honestly, as farfetched to some as it may sound, another one of my deceased mentors is Mother Teresa. Growing up, Grandma would talk about this woman, and in her description a martyr was a powerful thing to be. How could one claim that this blessed being suffered loneliness because she gave her life to God's work? I'm not worthy of the grace that I have been given. It isn't the opposite of empowerment to know that I

29

am not always. It empowers me with humility and the complete and utter knowledge that I am here to simply be a channel for that grace to touch others. Things of this world are not ours to hoard and keep merely for our own satisfaction. Neither are things such as grace and forgiveness. Even if I choose to remove someone from my life, it doesn't mean that I haven't forgiven. I have.

When I found out through Ed about the opportunity to go to Kenya, I was eager to hear more. My son, John, and I went to meet a wonderful man named Reegan, who spoke about the conditions of his own childhood in Kenya and how he got started with Zoe. Hearing him, I felt desperate to go and help. But I was really in awe at the way that Reegan showed such pride and strength. It was his number one thing to create safety and prosperity for the children of Africa who knew firsthand as he did the fear of being alone.

Because John was very young and I was unsure what he'd see in Kenya, I felt it best to only take Mary.

The journey to Kenya connected Mary and me to even more of the world. It further confirmed my passions. Mary and I—and the ten others, led by Zoe's leader, Greg—spent two weeks in Maua, a village in Kenya, where we learned about Zoe's orphan-empowerment program. Visiting sites where children had been left in horrible conditions of poverty gave my heart new focus. When the beat-up van came to a stop, we got out and gathered around a hut where three children lived and cared for one another because their parents had died. I was so overcome with love that I felt the need to embrace each one of the children. They were at first limp and unreceptive, but within seconds, one squeezed me, then another, and then the other. I tried to hold back the tears. They were tears of joy because the children knew we were there to help, and most importantly, they knew they were not alone—anymore.

Waking in the middle of the night to a strong burning smell, I opened the window to the building we were locked in and watched people around a metal can trying to stay warm. African nights are cold. Two people were fighting, and then one fell to the ground. Another couple was yelling at each other and a few children were playing and laughing. Sitting there, I was struck by the question of *why am I who I am*. Waking a few hours later to the aroma of breakfast, I brushed my teeth with a small supply of bottled water and put my hair up in the baseball cap that I'd brought. Mary greeted me at my door and smiled her beautiful smile. We were ready for a full day's work building a home and tarring a roof.

As with every meal I ate there, I felt guilty. We (the volunteers) were eating three meals a day when most of the population ate every third day, if that. But Reegan taught me not to think, at home or in Kenya, that I shouldn't eat this food because of my guilt over the starving children. "Stephanie," he said, "Do not feel badly about having food. Just be grateful and feel blessed when you have it." It has been one very crucial healing point for me with the struggle of my eating illness. Eat only what I need and by all means don't throw it up!

We were having a conversation about my health and why I couldn't eat in the first place, when I said, "Reegan, my body seems to reject food."

His soft smile always made me feel like I was in the presence of Jesus himself. "Stephanie, it is because you see food as your enemy, because of the way you have been raised to see mostly gluttony. We see it as life-sustaining and only eat that which keeps us alive, nothing more."

"I feel badly that I have food but don't want it."

Reegan got up to fill his plate with small amounts of rice and chicken. Putting his hand over mine, he said, "Then just eat it for the children you wish you could feed." And so I did. I was going to eat vicariously for all those children and adults we saw digging through the trash in the early morning for a meal. Ingenuity and survival were what defined the starving people of Africa.

All through life I've heard, "If not for the grace of God there go I." But not until that day did I fully comprehend the meaning of that phrase. Instead of feeling bewildered at why I wasn't someone who lived in this place and in these conditions, I decided that it had to be because I felt and saw what needed to be done. I would go home and talk about the needs here and find the needs in my own homeland as well. I realized that

Building a home in Kenya.

if I have been given a gift, then it was essential that I share it.

During the evenings in Kenya, after a tiring day of work on the site we were building, our group leader asked what our "God moment" was. Greg had us pick a moment in our day in which we saw the hand of God working. Describing it in detail to the rest of our team was a nightly ritual.

For me, that moment came during a meal that we shared with the staff of the Maua Methodist Hospital. We were covered head to toe in paint, dirt, and tar from the

work site. One of the hospital people announced that after introductions we would enjoy our meal. So we all sat up and put our forks down, ready to go through the mantra of where we lived and how this experience was touching us individually.

Empowering orphans in Kenya with Mary.

To our surprise, it was the local men and women who introduced themselves to us. Each of them worked daily to save lives and improve the health and well-being of the people of Kenya. But they actually took time out to meet the twelve of us and honor our presence. The hospital director went on about how they were our servants and put us on a pedestal, as he thanked us for being in their country. That is where the God moment started for me that day.

I could see that one of the men on our team looked almost angry.

He seemed very uncomfortable at the way this hospital director and his colleagues were thanking us for coming so far and do-ing so much for the people of Maua. Thank-ing us was fine, and we appreciated that,

Resting with Ana, the recipient of the home.

but I fully understood the feeling that I assumed was building inside my friend, Jon. When the intros were almost over, and we, too, had a chance to speak, Jon got to his feet and expressed a very different emotion.

He made it clear that we were the blessed ones. That being welcomed as if we were entitled to something was not warranted. Instead, he tried to make everyone in that room understand that we were servants to the needs of the people there.

We were called by a power greater than any of us—by God—to do what we could do to make a tiny difference. His words washed over me. In fact, they reflected what I had been thinking and I was grateful for his thoughts. Jon's tears made a huge impact on the people there, and I watched as each Kenyan and the others from all over the world sat up a bit straighter thanks to Jon's recognition and grace. I felt the same pride. We knew that we were the blessed ones there.

One of the lighter and even comical moments traveling the dirt roads was when our team went to church one Sunday. Having to go potty re-ally bad, I headed toward the woods. Once I found a private—or so I thought—spot I started to hike up my skirt. Standing there off in the distance was probably the oldest woman I'd ever seen. She walked my di-rection, shaking her head as I was rethinking my skirt hike. She motioned at the same time and pulled me to the hut that I knew held the toilet. I use the term "toilet" loosely here. I can now tell you from experience that

33

even if taught by an elderly village lady how to position yourself on the squat and potty, you might pee on yourself and her, too, and then the only thing to do is walk away together, laughing. Despite the language barriers of this world, we all have a common bond, and sometimes laughter is the best way to reinforce it. ☞

STEPHANIE HENRY

Stephanie Henry's life account is the type of story that demands to be told. After enduring a childhood shattered by molestation and neglect, Stephanie spent years battling drug use, eating disorders, a suicide attempt, a loss of child custody, and repeated incidents of domestic violence.

Driven to create better futures for victims around the world, Stephanie has partnered with several organizations to fight against physical and sexual abuse and human trafficking. Traveling to Guatemala, Cambodia, Mexico, Kenya and Rwanda, she has worked closely with the Saro Sary Foundation (SSF), the Love Life Foundation, ZOE Orphan Empowerment Program, and Guerrilla Aid.

Today Stephanie is an influential and inspirational speaker, author, and advocate who draws from her humanitarian efforts and extraordinary personal journey to give audiences an up-close view of the devastating effects of abuse as well as the opportunities for healing and recovery. Her powerful message of perseverance and inner strength and her call to action will remain with audiences long after they hear her speak.

Stephanie Henry-Ricchi
www.stephanieannhenry.com

Every Woman/Every Child

By Sheila Johnson

*M*y parents provided a warm, safe and loving home. There were five children and I was fortunate to be the youngest. We went to church Sundays and Wednesday nights. Little did I realize the strength I gained from growing up in a Christian home. This foundation prepared me for future challenges I would experience. Going to Sunday school with my friends, memorizing Bible verses, and Vacation Bible School in the summers was so much fun. It seemed like the teacher always called on me to pray—I would think "why me?" Today I think "Why not me". I thank my beautiful Mother, with so few resources, for the wisdom to make sure that I learned about Jesus. Today, I have no recollection of when I did not believe. I remember receiving my first Bible and I still have it. My favorite song was "This Little Light of Mine, I am going to let it Shine". School was also one of my favorite places to go. Education opened my mind to what could be. Sports taught me to think like a champion. Life on the farm was the early heartbeat on my road to wisdom.

There Are Times When You Should Move On

Growing up in a traditional home, I thought all men were like my father—responsible, caring and intelligent. He loved and respected my mother. What a lucky girl I was! However, at the age of 21 I found myself unhappily married and living in Dallas, Texas. It was a long way (65 miles) from my home town and psychologically it felt like a much greater distance. My little girl was only eighteen months old when I made a decision, for our safety, to divorce a physically abusive alcoholic. It was a frightening world and when I look back it appeared that I was not financially or emotionally prepared, but I knew God would show me the way. At that time there was no law in place in Texas to garnish wages on behalf of child support. So as a mother of a small child I asked myself," what do I do now?" I have to get a job that will provide for "all" of our needs. I was ashamed and embarrassed for my failed marriage. Consequently, asking for help was not an option. From an early age, my mother taught me to trust God and my father taught me to learn from my mistakes, move on and be responsible.

The Door Opens

My brother-in-law was an executive with a technology firm and arranged for a job interview. Ralph Waldo Emerson said, "What lies behind us and what lies before us are tiny matters compared to what lies within us". As I look back I truly see God's hand at work. This small entry-level job led to 20 years of the adventure of a lifetime for me. My boss became a co-founder of a major firm and was instrumental in my early success. In 1969 there were very few women in the technology industry in the US. It is reported that I was the first female to market semiconductors/microprocessors, subsequently opening the door for future women to enter this male-dominated industry.

An 8 to 5 job was not satisfying or challenging to me. The pay was also limited. One day I decided that sales were the answer. My income would only be limited by my efforts and by observing the sales men I figured that I could do just as well and I knew that I would work harder. I just picked up my briefcase, told the secretary, "see you later" and away I went on my first sales call. I figured, "so what if they fire me, I am only making peanuts and I can always find another job making peanuts." For some reason, my boss liked and believed in me. He not only promoted me to the sales department, he also provided a new company car and gave me an expense allowance. Wow, I had arrived!

I believe risk taking—being on the edge and willing to give it all and do it all, fully committed—is truly the key to success. However, on my first sales call at age 23 I remember fearfully asking God for help and guidance. Trusting God is essential.

To be the Guide You Must First Make the Journey

During this time I observed that some divorced Mothers were leaving their children in the care of their Grandparents and other people due to their limited finances. I loved my daughter dearly and was determined to give her all that I possibly could on my own. She had a great education, was involved in sports, music, art and her church. She was the reason for all my activities and I loved the responsibility. With the aid of student loans and grants I was able to send both of us to college. However, I learned that money will go just so far. There were only so many hours in the day. Along the way I certainly experienced corporate jealousy and learned how limiting it can be. I also experienced discrimination, but didn't dare mention the word or I would be out of a job. That part of the corporate game I learned reluctantly.

In the 80's, as a part of an employee pay plan, stock options were introduced and later 401k plans were offered. I began to familiarize myself with other income options. I became intrigued with the stock market.

Every Monday morning I would go to the library to study the most recent stock reports. There was no CNBC and I could not afford the Wall Street Journal. Looking outside my sales ability, I tried my hand at investing in stocks of companies that I understood. Realizing that the market does not care whether I am male or female I felt that I had a fair chance. Of course, I made some mistakes. However, I believe "to learn the game, you must be willing to play the game". Since I was young, time was on my side. If I made a mistake I had time to recoup my losses. Studying hard and working hard paid off and this was the beginning of my "nest egg".

When I was 30 years of age the president of a technology company approached me with "seed money" to start my own company. Being both flattered and surprised, I decided that he just might be right. It was a great opportunity and experience! It forced me once again to step out into unfamiliar territory. This is where I was tested and learned some great lessons —not only about the business world, but also about myself. Over time I was able to merge this company with a larger company, and eventually sold my interest. It is important that I share this story to demonstrate what can happen by just keep putting one foot in front of the other. Through a combination of doing the "right" things daily, good things happen. A fellow business associate, who I have known for many years told me, "you may not always be the most likeable person—but you are the go to girl because you can be trusted". This is a great compliment and has followed me throughout my career and personal life.

My Next Great Adventure

On March 31, 1989, I met my husband at a private party. It truly was love at first sight. He is my "hero" in many ways. He leads by example. For the first time, I met someone who believes in me, is not threatened by me and encourages me to be the best I can be. We married a year later and began to work together in the insurance and financial service industry. Fascinated by finance and combining my personal financial experience, becoming an investment professional was to become my next career. As of this writing Bob and I have been working together for 23 years. Perhaps one day we will jointly write a book about working and living with your spouse 24/7. Some days are more interesting than others. However, we love our clients and they are family to us.

Improving the Lives of Women and Children

My parents taught me the value of giving back. For years I contributed here and there, performed volunteer work and considered it enough. Seven years ago, after observing women's lack of financial knowledge, I decided to form a Women's Financial Study Group. It was very informal and non-threatening. My desire was to enlighten and empower women with choices in regard to the types of investment options available depending on their goals and time frame. My message to them is "You are safe. There is no shame and no blame". Being a daughter, mother, wife, employee, business owner—and simply just being a woman—I feel uniquely qualified to understand and help women in many financial areas. Being voted Class Treasurer three years in a row in high school is somewhat revealing.

Fashion and Finance

Sharing my passion for Women & Finance recently with a Futurist was an eye opener. She stated that this effort was a futile endeavor to change a culture— one in which men make most of the financial decisions and it is not likely to change. Additionally, she stated of all the Lunch &

Learns, Seminars, and one-on-one coaching, only 1% will "get it". At first I was angry, then sad—then I thought "so what, I'll take that 1%". Educating a woman has the power to change a nation. It is a start. "One voice can make a difference." Giving up is not an option for this author. At the time of this writing my broker/dealer, which is the largest insurance company in the world, has just implemented a new marketing segment titled the "I Generation". It is specifically defined as the independent woman. Perhaps the Futurist was wrong.

Over the years I have had the pleasure of working with many women from all walks of life. Words cannot express the joy I receive when we have developed a plan together with their needs in mind and I can see the hope in their eyes. One girl said to me "I stopped dreaming." Change and commitment can affect your life today and generations to come. I firmly believe that "Every Woman" should feel smart and confident when it comes to money and they have the right to access the information and tools that will enable them to become financially secure.

On September 11, 2009 Bob and I asked ourselves, "What can we do for those who give so much— police officers and firefighters"? As a result we co-founded the McKinney Public Safety Scholarship Foundation benefiting the children of the police and firefighters of our home town— McKinney, Texas.

Neither Bob's parents nor my parents could afford to send us to college. My parents never graduated from high school. Their goal was to raise five children and provide a high school education—which they did. When I graduated from high school, I was Salutatorian of my class and received a scholarship to a university in Dallas. However, I had no car and no means of income so the scholarship was unused. In my 20's I was able to send myself, and later my daughter, through college. Bob and I know first-hand the financial hardship and challenge of going to college while working full time. We also know the importance of an education.

The last four years the McKinney Public Safety Scholarship Foundation has awarded 42 scholarships to some very outstanding students.

2013 Scholarship

Their majors include: teaching, nursing, law, criminal justice, aviation, professional basketball, meteorology, sports medicine, pharmacy, veterinary medicine and custom home construction. The community has stepped up to help us and we now have long term commitments from a woman's organization, car dealerships, a home builder, realtors, a CPA, doctors, an orthodontist and several individuals who want to be a part of this great effort. We thank them.

Nelson Mandela stated: "Education is the most powerful weapon you can use to change the world"

I believe "Every Child" deserves an education! Bob and I saw a need and with the help of God working through others we are endeavoring to fill it. ☞

SHEILA JOHNSON

Outstanding in her community for being a devoted advocate for "Financial Education and Guidance for Women", Sheila Johnson holds a 6 & 63 Security License, Insurance License, is a Registered Representative and is the Managing Partner of Johnson Insurance & Financial—a Boutique Financial Service Company since 1969. She is a 2010, 2011 and 2012 recipient of the Million Dollar Round Table award for her performance and was voted one of the Top Business Women by the Chamber of Commerce in McKinney 2010 and 2011. She was also voted Best Insurance Agent for 2012. Sheila and her husband, Bob, founded a Scholarship Foundation benefiting the children of the McKinney Police and Firefighters. She created a CD, "Smart Women/Safe Money". This year she received the Love Life Foundation—"Women Who Serve Award". Sheila is a published author, provides one-on-one tutoring, Lunch & Learn Events and encourages women to identify their passion (what is in their hearts). She states," A Financial Plan will not only affect your life but also generations to come. This is your Precious Life and your Dreams matter".

www.JohnsonInsuranceandFinancial.com,
7290 Virginia Pkwy, Suite 2500, McKinney, TX 75071
214.726.0000
email: Sheila@johnsoninsuranceandfinancial.com.

My Valentine's Day Story

By Angela Paxton

I've always loved Valentine's Day. I know that I'm not alone: it's special to many people for many different reasons. Some celebrate proposals, some anniversaries, and most the simple opportunity to say "I love you" to someone dear. But for me, Valentine's Day—this day of celebrating love—is my birthday, and it has always seemed profoundly fitting. You see, I am an adopted child, and Valentine's Day is the story of my life.

I never remember being told that I was adopted. I just knew, the same way other children know they are natural children of their parents. And I knew it was a special thing. I grew up knowing that I was chosen. I knew that my birth mother had been an unmarried college student, and I lived in gratitude for her noble choice to give me a life in a family with a loving mother and father. My younger brother was adopted two years after me.

I was born in New Braunfels, but I grew up in Rendon—a small, still-unincorporated Texas town south of Fort Worth. My mom, Anita, my dad, Wayne, my brother, Corey, and I went to church every Sunday morning, Sunday night and Wednesday night. My parents attended (and

Mhy adopted family, 1967: brother, Corey; father, Wayne; me; mom, Anita. They don't make hair like that anymore!

sometimes coached!) every volleyball, basketball and softball game I ever played, were on the front row for every piano recital and church solo, and used their yearly vacation time to voluntarily chaperone my youth group mission trips. I grew up with friends who loved me no matter what and challenged me to be my best and follow God with all my heart. I graduated third in my class at Mansfield High School and went to Baylor University on a scholarship. There I realized that I really liked math, began taking my love of music seriously, and made lifelong friends. My senior year at Baylor—and just in time, I might add—I fell in love with the student body president, Ken Paxton. We married the following year on the only open weekend of Baylor football season and finished out our honeymoon at Baylor Homecoming.

We began married life in Houston, where I pursued a master's degree in education at the University of Houston – Clear Lake. We then moved to Charlottesville, Virginia, where I coached and taught high school and middle school and Ken received his law degree from the University of Virginia School of Law. After three years, we returned to Texas. Ken began his law career and I continued to teach school until we began our family. Tucker, Abby and Mattie were all born in Dallas. Two days after Mattie was born we moved to McKinney to help start a church, and Katie was born two years later.

August of 2002 found us approaching the first of Ken's elections to five terms in the Texas House of Representatives and a term in the Texas Senate. Our children were three, five, seven and nine. Ken and I were both on the verge of our fortieth birthdays. Ken had just launched into solo law practice and I was engaged in our church's women's ministry and sang on the worship team. Life was exciting and busy and about as unpredictable as it had ever been. But it was about to become even more so.

That August, an unexpected letter arrived with all of the election-related mail addressed to Ken. It was a certified letter addressed to me. Not recognizing the return address, I opened the envelope and read the letter, which began:

> *Dear Angela Suzanne Paxton,*
>
> *I am a birth mother searching for my first child who was born February 14, 1963 in New Braunfels, Texas.*

It wasn't that I had never been curious. But I had long ago decided to be comfortable with the mystery inherent in being an adopted child. My father had once confided with me my mother's secret fear that my brother and I might not see her as our "real" mother. I had no desire to contribute to that fear by seeking out my birth parents. Her peace of mind in that regard weighed in more heavily than curiosity ever could.

But I had always longed to tell my birth mother thank you. In fact, in 2000 I had written a song to my unknown birthmother and called it "A Thank You Song (for Linda)." I'm not sure why I gave her a name in my notes, but I did.

So you can only imagine my surprise when I saw how the letter concluded:

> *I hopefully wait to hear from you.*
>
> *Sincerely,*
>
> *Linda*

A few weeks later, with my mom's blessing, I met Linda face to face. I

My birth-grandmother, Mattie Rena, and my birth-mother, Linda.

sang the song I had written for her to her. We cried. We laughed. My children welcomed a new grandmother into their lives ("Grand-Birth mother," was the title our son, Tucker, bequeathed to her) and Ken acquired a second mother-in-law. At the age of 39, I met four brothers and sisters I had never known along with aunts and uncles and cousins. They told me, "We have been praying that the Lord would bring you back to us." I met my grandmother, Mattie Rena. Ken and I marveled together that five years before we knew her, we had named our third child, Mattie, after her!

Although my mother had encouraged me to meet my birth family, she privately struggled. For two years she resisted the invitation to meet Linda, my birth mother and her feared "competition." And then suddenly, my mom announced: "I'm ready to meet Linda."

And so it was that in the spring of 2004 in a hotel room at a women's retreat, I witnessed something I never dreamed I would see. I watched my birth mother present my mother with a dozen red roses, kneel before her and say, "Thank you. You gave Angela what I never could have given her. You gave her a life." And then I watched my mom, who had

My birth-mother, Linda, and my mom, Anita with the famous roses.

been unable to conceive a child, reply through tears, "No, thank you— you gave her what I never could have—you gave her life." And we all cried smiling tears as one woman's lifelong fear melted into a miraculous friendship.

I have witnessed healing that I never expected to see. When my birth grandmother—the woman who made the decision that I would be adopted—accepted me into her life with open arms, her daughter—my birth-mother—felt accepted again, healing a deep though hidden pain of rejection. My adopted mother, after so many years of fear, was set free. In fact, when her health began declining and she came to live with us for five years, it was my birth mother—and her friend—who stayed with her for 10 days so our family could go on a vacation.

And that's why I've always loved Valentine's Day. It's not only my birthday; it truly is the story of my life. *Psalm 16:6* says, "The boundary lines have fallen for me in pleasant places; surely I have a delightful inheritance." Indeed, I have lived in love all of my life because the goodness of God put two very special women in my life: one who gave life to me, and one who gave me a life. ☞

ANGELA PAXTON

An adopted child, Angela Paxton grew up with a great awareness of the power of the love of God through the people in her life. She met Ken Paxton, her husband of 27 years, at Baylor University, where she earned a BA in Mathematical Science. She also holds a MS in Education and serves as a Guidance Counselor at Legacy Christian Academy in Frisco, Texas. Her husband, Ken, has served in the Texas Legislature since 2003 as a State Representative and State Senator. Angela and Ken have four children: Tucker, Abby, Mattie, and Katie. Active in women's ministry, Angela has served as a worship leader, helped found a "Mom-to-Mom" ministry, and encouraged countless women to spend time with God through her "Come Away" series. Angela is a former board member of Dallas Pregnancy Resource Center and Golden Corridor Republican Women.

The granddaughter of a Baptist music minister, Angela grew up with a deep appreciation of encountering God through the music of the church. A singer and songwriter, her songs, "Always" and "A Thank You Song (For Linda)" honor her adopted mother, Anita, and birth mother, Linda, respectively.

Angela Paxton
Speaker, Singer/Songwriter
website: AngelaPaxton.com
email: Angela@AngelaPaxton.com

Purpose, Enthusiasm, Perseverance

By Judy L. Pogue

*I*n our company, we call this PEP, because it motivates us to remember all three things that keep us on track. Purpose defines why we do what we do, enthusiasm energizes us to keep excited and motivated, and perseverance helps us remember that tough times don't last forever, but with God's help tough people do.

In 1979 my husband Paul and I borrowed $1,000 to start a small construction company. We had no idea that our modest beginning would blossom into a multi-million dollar business. We never dreamed that we would work in 58 different school districts and for a total of 64 different owners, and that many would be repeated through the years. We never dreamed that we would work on projects ranging from Texas A&M University to Collin County College. We never dreamed that we would build many of our local schools such as McKinney Boyd and several middle schools and elementary schools and police and fire stations, right here in our own community. We also never dreamed that we would be able to construct a facility like Prosper High School or Allen Performing Arts Center and the new

Allen Football Stadium. We never dreamed that we would have articles written in the Dallas News,

Pogue Construction Building

USA Today and Wall Street Journal, and New York Times, but our great and mighty God knew when he planted the vision in our heart. Paul and I have always set goals for our family, our business and our ministry every New Year's Day. The Bible specifically says "where there is no vision the people perish". I believe that you must set goals and have realistic ways to reach them.

In 1991 we moved our family to McKinney, Texas and to our home that we affectionately call "Shenandoah Ranch". Five years later, Pogue Construction moved from Sherman, Texas and located in the City of McKinney. We did most of our work in Collin County and in the North Texas and Dallas area, so this move made sense. Our entire family knew it was a God move. Our sons attended school in McKinney and graduated from McKinney High School before they attended Texas A&M in College Station. We love our city, because the people in our community are kind and generous. Our friends that we have developed, personally and through our construction company, are what we call our "treasures". These friends have stood with us through good times and bad times and we will be forever grateful for their love and support. We live in a great city. We believe that we are responsible to learn, earn, and return.

The word stewardship is very important to our family. When my husband and I were first married we made a commitment to tithe 10% of our income. The *Bible* says in *Malachi 3*, "Bring all the tithes to the storehouse and that God will open the windows of heaven upon you and pour out such a blessing that there will not be room to receive all of it". I am a living breathing testimony of such blessing. There have been some extremely lean times in owning a company over three decades. We have had recessions and stock market downturns, and many people have suffered. Our difference is that we never confessed it; we believed that in God's economy there is always enough. We never missed a paycheck, and neither did our employees. If you study the *Bible*, it tells a story of how Isaac sowed in a famine and reaped a 100 fold, this is found in *Gen. 6:12*. One of my husband's favorite scriptures is *Phil. 4:19* that states "My God shall supply all my needs according to His riches in glory." The other scriptural truth we have stood on is *Matt. 6:33*, "But seek first the kingdom of God and his righteousness and all these things shall be added to you". We have to make God a priority in our life. This includes our daily walk with God, our family, and in our business. We cannot separate our earthly life from our spiritual life. We are body, soul, and spirit. Most of our problems and poor decisions come from simply not putting God first. Many times we can get so busy, we forget to pray. I have been very moved by a book called "Circle Maker" by Mark Batterson. In this book, he encourages you to pray and never give up on your dreams. He encourages you to hit your knees first thing, and ask God to interrupt your day and fill you with wisdom and discernment. There is incredible power in having the proper priorities in your life.

Through so many difficult times in our life we would stop and consult God. This is where our purpose, enthusiasm, and perseverance statement would keep us from giving up.

There will be many times in your life that you will hit obstacles. There is a saying "you make lemonade out of lemons". When you have faith that God truly does work even the bad things for our good, then you can have hope for tomorrow. There are several things we do as a family when the challenges of our life come our way. I can give you an example of what I did as a woman who knows the power of prayer. A few years ago, we were blindsided by a court battle that we never expected or deserved. This process lasted several years, and it was extremely difficult on our family and our business. Many times in our life difficult times come and go and pass by very quickly. This one did not. God put such faith in my heart that I knew without a shadow of a doubt we would be victorious. *Psalms 34:19* "Many are the afflictions of the righteous, but God delivers them out of them all". I stood believing for our business and our family. I wrote scriptures and I put them all over the house, in the closet, in the bedroom, in the kitchen, in the garage and in my car. *Proverbs 3:3* tells us to "write them on the tablet of your heart". We know as Christians that God spoke the world into existence by His words, and since we have His spirit within us, we can do the same. We also did not speak negative words. This is where we remembered our purpose. As a family, we stood on God's written word, we spoke positively, we looked forward to the future and we persevered. God's grace is so amazing, and His love is overwhelming and endless. Only God can turn things around and make disappointments turn into the best thing that could ever happen to us. God has a plan, and his ultimate plan is that He gets all the Glory and people see your testimony through the most difficult challenges of your life. Many times in the Bible, the disciples were tested and went through perilous days, but God always had a purpose. Sometimes it is not what you did wrong, it is what you did right. God will allow tribulation and trials to come your way if it serves a higher purpose. The higher purpose is always about turning hearts to God. God gave us a great victory, because we trusted in Him and persevered.

We are on a great journey and it should be filled with wonder and surprise. Our great God has a plan for our lives and all we have to do is, seek Him and find the strategies for our future. You should wake up every morning with joy and excitement, knowing that He made this day for you to rejoice. I pray all the time for great surprises, and most of the time I get them. I know I am a daughter of a King, and that nothing I do can ever separate that love from me. I am challenged every time I read the book of *Esther*. Our *Bible* study recently went through six weeks of study. In this book, Mordecai says to Esther "who knows if you have not attained royalty for such a time as this". He challenges Esther to be mindful that God has allowed all that has happened to her to be used for His Glory to save her people. I believe as people of God it is not time to be silent any longer. We have let things happen in our nation that would break the hearts of our founders of our nation. We must be bold and stand for our families and for our nation. God wants us to pray and turn our country back to the principles of faith and freedom that our great nation was founded on. The message I personally feel so strongly about is a challenge to wake up a sleeping nation. We have slumbered too long, and our children and children's children need us to be serious about the things of God. It is not too late. Maybe we need more than a revival, we need a spiritual revolution. It starts with you and me, having the courage and the perseverance to dedicate ourselves to putting God first in every area of our life. We need to be asking bold prayers and not to give up until we hear from God. I am thankful I had a praying mother and grandmother who prayed for me continually. I believe their prayers are still being answered.

One of the key words in our mission statement is purpose. It can be defined as "the reason for which anything is done, created or exists. I understand this story is about my life, but after 38 years of marriage it is impossible to separate it from my dear husband, Paul. His purpose is truly giving. When he was a young boy he wanted to be a missionary in Africa. He was the youngest of nine children, and his father died when he was seven. He has a story that would be a best seller and maybe someday he will write it. His life was full of hardships and challenges. The greatest gift he had in his life was a praying mother named "Gracie". She loved her family and even started a little church in her kitchen that is still in existence today. Paul went to church every Sunday, Sunday night, Wednesday night, special services and week-long revivals. We have this in common because my parents had me in church that often, too. We have often talked about how we both grew up to love the old hymns of the church, such as *Amazing Grace, Great is Thou Faithfulness,* and *Blessed Assurance*. Paul and I both felt a call for missions at a young age. So let me turn back the clock 30 years. Paul and I had finally saved enough money to take a trip. We looked to see how far we could go with the money we had. Our decision and our money came down to Mexico. While in Mexico we saw the beautiful mountains and the turquoise blue ocean with the sparking white sand, but we saw something else. We saw our purpose. As we were driving along a stretch of highway for several hundred miles we saw the people. We saw people bathing in the river, we saw children with no clothes and no shoes. We saw hunger and poverty. Our hearts were so impacted that even as we were flying home we thought about a way to help these precious people. If not for God and His divine plan, it could be us and our children.

In the next couple of weeks, at our church, I met a woman named Mary Lou Myers. She told me that her husband was a missionary to Mexico, and she invited us to dinner at her home to meet him. What can I say about Larry Myers of Mexico Ministries? There is not enough time, but I will tell you what I can. At our first meeting he told us how God had called him to leave a thriving church and go to the mission field in Mexico. Unfortunately, the denomination he was with didn't agree and didn't support him. Again we are talking about purpose. If God has a plan he will supply all your needs.

Larry Myers packed up and went into the villages and huts and began to preach the gospel. He shared the love of God and stayed in thatched huts full of rats and mud, but he persevered. He began to share his story of the faithfulness of God and how he was building a church and later a hospital on the same highway we had just traveled in Mexico. In fact, we were only about 100 yards from where construction was starting on the church. We were amazed and felt that vision coming to pass in our hearts. A few months later, we were back on that same highway walking on the property in the mountains and staring up at the beautiful mango trees, and smelling the aroma of all the coffee bean plants. We knew we had found our purpose. Our construction company began to grow, and every time we had any extra money it went to Mexico Missions. Paul went on every mission trip he could. He would work and save money and go with Larry Myers to all parts of Mexico and small villages few people will ever see. These were hard trips in some dangerous parts of Mexico. They would mix cement by hand and pour it by shovels. In many villages, they had no electricity or running water. They would do construction with their bare hands for eight to 12 hours a day. This was a season for me to pray and to study God's word. In the early years, I was limited on my mission trips because we had young sons at home. As a wife, I learned to pray and encourage my husband to follow God's plan. It is very important to know that you will go through seasons of your life. In every season of your life you are growing and you are learning something valuable. When you are a young mother at home sometimes you can get discouraged. However, it is important to remember that this time with your children is extremely important. Your time will come if you are faithful to do first things first. I remember hearing in my heart God saying that if I would love my husband and be faithful and teach my children the word of God I would truly be blessed all the days of my life. After all these years, I have never regretted my decision to support and believe in my husband. Anyway, as Mexico Ministries began to grow, so did Pogue Construction. Many times while Paul was building a church in Mexico, he would get a new job. We were so blessed to have amazing employees that knew we were more than just a construction company; we were a ministry, too. Every time we gave an offering, God would bless us with a new project. It matters who you partner with. There are divine relationships and alignments that only God could put together. Many people have blessed us along the way, but there will never be another person that has impacted our lives such as Larry Myers.

Paul and Judy Pogue on Mission Trip to Chiapas, Mexico.

We have so many stories of lives that have been touched through our mission work. One story is about a man named Fabanio. Paul and Larry Myers found out that he had a small little shack where he held church services every Sunday in Tuxtla Gutierrez. The little hut was covered with newspapers and cardboard. One day after visiting, Paul and Larry said: "we are going to build you a church". I am sure Fabanio thought *there's no way it can happen*. As Paul, Larry and Fabanio were hiking down from the hillside from the little shack, Fabanio pulled up his slacks and told them he only had one leg. He told them the story that when he was younger, he was in the Mexican Army and he had lost his leg jumping off a train. He was in the hospital for nine months. During that time, his wife prayed that he would live and give his heart to God and that's exactly what happened. When we went back to see the new beautiful church with white painted walls and beautiful flowers growing, he was so happy. I will never forget that he said "It was worth the pain". Now he has a new beautiful church and a loving family with a purpose to preach the gospel. Mexico Ministries was able to build that church and turn over the keys to him with no debt. It's a wonderful feeling to partner with people who know their purpose. There are so many things you can do for people when you are blessed to be a blessing.

Another thing I have learned that as a Christian you bring in the blessing. One of my favorite passages in the *Bible* is *Deut. 28: 1-14.* This chapter describes the blessing of God. It tells us we are blessed in the city, we are blessed in the country, our livestock is blessed, and our children are blessed. You are blessed when you come in and when you go out. The Lord will cause your enemies to be defeated before you, and your storehouses will overflow. Now I think that is a great word for all of us. So my story is about Rosa, she is a mother of five and loves God with all of her heart. She lives high in the mountains in Chiapas, Mexico. When we first met her she lived in one room with a dirt floor. The blessing is on her—now she has a three-story house and running water. Her son is the local pastor and he is building a new church that will seat several hundred people on top of the mountain. A clinic is located next door to her house, and we have a paid doctor that treats patients from all over the region free of charge.

Purpose drives you, but enthusiasm keeps you motivated. Several years ago we became acquainted with the orphanage called Casa Hogar Alegra. The name means House of Hope. They rescue abused and abandoned children. Many of the children are found on the streets looking for food. When you look at the smiles on these children's faces you are excited and enthused. For several years, we have been involved in helping the orphanage with their needs. We have helped with books, computers, ovens for baking bread, water facilities, bedding, a chapel and many other projects. Our most memorable experience each December is when we take over 100 orphans shopping. We take a team from the US and load the children in vans and busses and give them Christmas blessings. We assign several children, hopefully with a translator if needed, and shop until we drop. You can imagine how those little smiles and hugs motivate you to follow your purpose. That day they pick out clothes, pajamas, underwear, socks and shoes. Then to top off the day we take them to Burger King or McDonald's. You should see the workers in the restaurant when we tell them we need 40 Happy Meals at a time, and by the way please get your ice cream machine ready! This year we were able to buy a projector so that they could have Disney movies on the weekends. We have watched them grow and they are well loved and cared for. Elizabeth Castelazo Noguera is the director of the orphanage, and she is truly a saint to dedicate her life so unselfishly to these precious children. I promise if you ever take a trip with us to this orphanage you will know purpose, enthusiasm, and perseverance.

In the last couple of years, we have made some changes in our business. Paul is refocusing on his mission's trips and his local non-profit organization called Minuteman Disaster Relief. Our younger son is now CEO of Pogue Construction. We believe God will empower him to take the company to the next level. Brandon, our middle son, owns The Pogue Group Commercial Real-estate and Development Company. Randy owns Pogue Engineering and is now on the McKinney City Council. All three sons go on missions' trips, and I am happy to say they are all givers as well. They have a reputation of knowing how to learn, earn, and return.

The Pogues with their grandchildren.

God has given us wonderful godly daughter-in-laws, and eight of the most beautiful grandchildren you have ever seen. We trust that God will continue the legacy of the Pogue Family through their lives. It is a blessing that they all live and work in McKinney. One of our greatest joys is when the grandchildren come to Mimi's and Poppy's house. We get lots of hugs and kisses.

So to sum it up, we are living like our favorite movie "It's a Wonderful Life". We still continue to support pre-K children and an orphanage in Kenya as well as an accredited seminary and an elementary school in India. I am writing a book and working on my international women's conferences called "Esther's Arise." Our plans for next year include several women's *Bible* studies and a conference to empower women. I want to leave a legacy for my children and children's children. My desire is that they will be a testimony of God's blessing and favor on their life. I love the scripture *Proverbs 20:7* "the righteous walks in his integrity and his children are blessed after him."

Remember God loves you; He gave His life so you could live victorious. Dare to dream again, let God take you places you have never been. You have a story waiting to be told. Life goes very fast, enjoy the journey. You have been blessed to be a blessing. ☞

JUDY POGUE

Looking back over the 30 year history of Pogue Construction, Judy and her husband can see the fingerprints of God. They borrowed $1,000 to start the business over three decades ago. Pogue Construction is now one of the largest commercial construction companies in North Texas. Many of the schools in McKinney and surrounding areas have been built by their company. Judy believes that they have been blessed to be a blessing. For over 30 years, they have partnered together in international missions in Mexico, India, Africa and Nicaragua. Judy has taught women's Bible studies at her home, in McKinney Texas called "Shenandoah Ranch" for over ten years. She is now leading women conferences locally and in different parts of the world. Judy recently returned from the Dominican Republic where a team of women taught an "Esther Arise" conference, sponsored by "Global Advance". Judy's passion is to empower women to know their authority through Christ. Her message is to inspire women to dream big dreams, and to understand that nothing is impossible with God. Every Christmas Judy and her husband, Paul, partner with Mexico Ministries and clothe and feed over 100 orphans in Tuxtla Gutierrez, Mexico. They have a non-profit charity called "Pogue Family Missions" to help people in need around the world.

She started singing at the young age of five years old, and gave her life to Christ at seven. In her earlier years, she lived in Miami, Florida and was a professional singer.

She has served as President of the McKinney High School PTO, Heard Museum Board, and the McKinney Education Board for ten years. She is now serving on the executive board of "Christ for India". Judy has been married to Paul Pogue for over 38 years. They have three grown sons and eight grandchil-

dren. All three of their sons and families own businesses and live in McKinney, Texas.

Judy Pogue
Judy L. Pogue
Pogue Construction/Motivational Speaker
www.pogueconstruction.com
Judy@pogueconstruction.com

Difference Makers Don't Procrastinate

By Michelle Prince

I truly believe that most people want to do well in this world and make a positive impact in their communities, families and around the world. I believe that we all want to be "Difference Makers."

I first heard the term "Difference Maker" when I was in my twenties working for Zig Ziglar. It was a part of the company's mission statement and it made a lasting impression on me. "To be a difference maker in the personal, family and business lives of enough people to make a positive difference in America and the World." Having seen Mr. Ziglar live that mission made me want to do the same, so I made it my goal in life to become a "Difference Maker" too.

What is the secret to becoming a "Difference Maker?" It's a combination of many things such as finding your purpose, living with passion, overcoming obstacles and much more but it starts with taking action! It starts with defining specific goals for your life and making a plan to accomplish them!

Zig Ziglar was a big proponent of setting goals. He was always asking:

Austin, Tyler, Michelle & Chris Prince

What do you want to be? What do you want to do? What do you want to have? I have learned a lot from his leadership. In the Prince household, we have a tradition around setting goals. (I'll admit right now that I may have forced this tradition at first, since I am the one who is into personal development in our family.) Every New Year's Eve, we gather around, and each of us gets a piece of paper to write down five personal goals for the coming year—five things we want to be; five things we want to do; five things we want to have. We all do this, even my kids.

We started this tradition when my oldest son was four years old. Their goals when they were little were kind of sweet and funny sometimes. They would list things like going roller skating, making the soccer team, or going to Disney World. But throughout the year, when they would accomplish one of their goals, we would go to their room where the list was posted and check that goal off the list. It gave all of us a terrific sense of accomplishment.

We repeated the exercise as a family, too. As a family, what do we want to be? What do we want to do? What do we want to have? We worked toward our collective goals and grew as a family.

When my son was six years old, he said something that completely blew me away. It was the day he realized he had met all five goals he had written down for the year.

"Mom, this is so cool!" he said. "All you have to do is write it down, and it happens!"

I got such a kick out of that. We tend to complicate things so much as adults, but this little six year old got it. It was that simple. All we have to do is figure out what we want and write it down. Then, it is much more likely to happen.

Now, back to the topic of goals, I have a question for you. Why do some people accomplish their goals and others don't?

I am asked this question all the time, and there are many answers.

There are some people who just refuse to take the time to set goals. They think they already know what they want in life, so they shouldn't have to write it down. I can tell you from my years of coaching experience, those are typically the people who don't accomplish any of their goals.

Other people create goals, but their goals are not really tied to their passion or purpose in life. That is exactly why I think it is so important to first discover your passions before you do anything else. If you're not setting goals around something you are truly passionate about, what are the chances that you will achieve those goals? You have to tie that in and make sure that you look at it very closely before you set your goals.

Another reason that people do not accomplish their goals is that they set a goal and never look at it again. I have been guilty of this—I set a goal, put it in the drawer, and then forget about it for months. The goal has to be in a place where you will see it every day, so that you can maintain your focus on achieving it.

There are many, many reasons why people do not achieve their goals, but one reason surpasses all the rest: procrastination.

Procrastination is such a prevalent barrier to reaching your goals. When I speak to groups, I often ask, "How many of you are procrastinators?"

You wouldn't believe the response! People are practically climbing over their chairs to claim this ailment—as if they're proud of it. It's nothing to be proud of, though.

We act like procrastination is some sort of disease that we cannot fight. However, think about other aspects of your life. Did you procrastinate checking your email this morning? Did you procrastinate going on *Twitter* or *Facebook*? Probably not.

But are you procrastinating getting your work done? What about taking that trip you have always wanted to take? Procrastination is a choice, and we tend to reserve it for the big things. We procrastinate on the things that matter the most; the things that will bring the most joy and satisfaction. It's really silly when you think about it, but that's what we do. We put the important things on the back burner.

Let me tell you, your days of procrastinating are numbered. You are no longer going to wait for someday. I will walk you through a plan right now that will help you overcome procrastination and start making a difference NOW!

Step 1: Identify what's holding you back.

There are legitimate reasons why some people procrastinate. They may have difficulty concentrating or other physical or mental hurdles to overcome. But for most of us, that's not the case.

You might be procrastinating because of fear. Fear of failure, of course, but also fear of succeeding. If you accomplish this goal, then what?

Think about why you are procrastinating. Is it fear? Anxiety? What is holding you back? You have to identify it before you can remove it. Ask yourself: Why am I procrastinating on this? Do I not believe in myself? Do I think I'm not worth it? What is the negative jabber in my head around this? Am I getting anything positive out of putting this off?

Step 2: Practice discipline and motivation.

The simple truth is that achieving anything worthwhile in your life takes practice. If someone comes up to you and tells you they have an easy way for you to make a million dollars with almost no effort, run! You can achieve anything you want, but it's going to take some work.

That doesn't mean it has to be hard, though.

When you are following your goals and working on something you're passionate about, it doesn't feel like work. It's not hard, because you're right where you want to be.

When I wrote my book, *Winning in Life Now*, I got the inspiration for the book at a live event. I'm a big believer in live events, because being around other people is inspiring. I made the decision at that event to write my book.

So I went home, got out my laptop, and started cranking out that book. In three weeks, I had the entire thing written. Now, it took eight months to get all of the final pieces in place, but the big push only took three weeks. During that time, I stayed up later than I've ever stayed up; I got up earlier than I ever have before; I worked harder than I have ever worked in my life—and I had a full-time job on top of all this! And of course, motherhood never takes a break, either, so I was one busy woman.

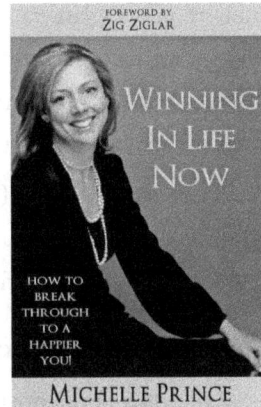

Winning In Life Now

It didn't matter. I was working very, very hard, but it wasn't difficult, because the project was pulling me, rather than me pushing the project. It was exhilarating.

If you choose a goal that is aligned with your passion, you will have the same experience. You will have to practice and develop a strong discipline and motivation, but it will not be hard, because your heart will be in it.

Step 3: Dust off your dreams.

What do you think would happen if I stood in front of a classroom of kindergarten students and asked them, "What do you want to be when you grow up? What are your dreams?"

They wouldn't hesitate to give their answers. Kids have dreams—big dreams—and they have every intention of making those dreams come true.

Do you remember your dreams? Have you thought about them lately? Dust off those old dreams, if they haven't been out in the light for awhile. Take a second look at them. They will rekindle your passion and help you to move forward in achieving your goals.

I caught a glimpse of my dream when I went to that Zig Ziglar seminar at age eighteen. I didn't even know what passion was back then, but something fired up inside of me when I was around people, successful people, who wanted more out of life. I am just as enthusiastic about this dream today as I was at eighteen.

So remind yourself of your passions. Dust off those dreams, and set goals to achieve them. Nothing strikes procrastination down faster than a passionate person with goals and plans to achieve their dreams.

Step 4: Start living now.

This one is deceptively simple, but procrastination really boils down to one thing: inaction. If you start living now, you launch into action and thwart evil procrastination. You have to make a conscious decision that you are worth it and then just do it. No waiting. No putting it off. Start living now! Why would you want to wait to realize your dreams and live your passion every day?

I would like to tell you a story about my friend Tom. I also included this story in my book Winning in Life Now, because I feel it is such an important illustration.

*T*om was in his early forties. He had it all: a wonderful family, young kids in elementary school and a beautiful wife. He was one of those guys who just seemed to do everything right. He ate right, worked out and took good care of himself. He did it all.

When Tom went to his annual doctor's appointment, his doctor discovered a little lump. They did a bunch of tests, and everything was just a bit off.

"Don't worry about it," the doctor assured him. "I'm sure it's fine. But let's just do a few more tests to be certain."

About a week later, Tom and his wife received a phone call from the doctor asking them to come back into the office. It didn't sound like he would be giving them terrific news, but nothing could have prepared them for what they heard that day. Not only did Tom have cancer, but it was in Stage IV, and he had six months to live. Six months.

What do you do with that diagnosis?

At first, Tom was mad. He flew through all of the stages of grief.

"This isn't fair!" he ranted. "How could this be happening to me? I did everything right!"

Then the sadness kicked in. "I have kids and a wife. What will happen to my beautiful family when I'm no longer here? I will miss seeing my children grow up. I will not get to grow old with my wife."

And finally, he came to acceptance. He realized that no matter what he did in that moment, he could not avoid the fact that there was a very good chance he would not be around in a few months.

That's when Tom made a decision. He said, "I'm only going to do the things I really, really love to do, and I'm going to spend whatever days I have left with the people I love the most."

That's exactly what he did. He spent time with his family, enjoying every minute with them. Another thing he loved to do was write. He had put it aside when life got busy with work and family, but in these final months, he started writing at night after his kids went to bed. He wrote letters and stories about what he did with them when they were young. He collected all of those wonderful memories in his words, so that his family could cherish them. It was a legacy that would become very valuable to them in the years to come.

Tom died six-and-a-half months after that doctor's appointment. His family was understandably devastated to lose him, but Tom's wife said something to me at the funeral that has stuck with me ever since. It is something that still inspires me to keep going after my goals and do what I love to do.

She said, "Tom came to me about a week before he died and said that he was grateful for the prognosis, because without it he never would have experienced what it really feels like to live."

That hit me right between the eyes. Why do we need a prognosis of death to get over whatever is holding us back? Why do we need somebody to tell us we're sick before we decide that it's okay to follow our dreams and goals?

Don't wait until you receive a fatal prognosis before you decide to get busy and live. You have an opportunity right now to launch into action, and that is exactly my point when it comes to overcoming procrastination. There is nothing in the world that is more important than your dreams and your goals. But you do have to take action and make it happen. At the end of the day, all you have to do is get started. Take one step.

What works for you may not work for someone else, so you have to find your own path. I had to get away from it all. I took a day off of work and got away from the distractions of family and business and everything else.

That's when I sat down and asked myself, "What do I really want out of life?" In the stillness, I was able to answer.

Start journaling; write down your ideas. Answer the questions I gave you earlier. Find out what it is you want, and then make a commitment to go after it.

There is one thing that many of us never fully realize: you are in control. You make choices every moment that put you exactly where you are today. If you want to be somewhere else, make different choices. You may not particularly like that statement, but the point is, no matter what is going on in your life, you have control over your attitude and your actions. What do you want to accomplish? Find out, and then get busy!

Make a commitment to follow your dreams. If you feel held back by responsibilities at work or at home, I urge you to make the commitment anyway—on behalf of your family and your business. You are much more valuable to everyone around you if you are leading a life that inspires them. So if you can't do it for yourself, do it for your family. When you inspire them, they will find the courage to follow your lead.

That's what happened to me when I wrote my first book. Sure, I was proud of the achievement of publishing a book, but there was so much more. I actually changed my kids' lives and so many others who were around me when I accomplished this goal. It had nothing to do with the content of the book. It was because I took action. I put one foot in front of the other and achieved a significant goal in my life. That inspired them to do the same.

You can do this, too. You can inspire others. You can be a "Difference Maker." Just make a commitment to yourself. If you can't do that, make a commitment to somebody else. Decide that you are done waiting and that you will go after your goals today.

I'm not special. I'm no different than you. I'm a wife, a mom, a friend, a sister; I have a company; I'm busy; I work. So if I can do it, you can do it. And I really truly believe that.

Life is so short. We all have an opportunity to be extraordinary. Don't wait until it's too late to grab on to your opportunity. Don't be ordinary. Take action. Overcome your procrastination, and make this year the best of your life. Be the "Difference Maker" you were born to be. ⌖

MICHELLE PRINCE

As a best-selling author, Zig Ziglar Motivational Speaker, business owner of multiple companies, wife of 15 years and mother of two young boys, Michelle Prince had to learn the art of juggling her personal and professional life successfully. Most people are juggling too many things, procrastinating and not getting as much done as they want, which leads to a life of frustration and unfulfilled goals. Michelle is passionate about helping people live with purpose, follow their passion and take action in big ways!

Michelle's passion ignited at the tender age of 18 when she met her mentor, Zig Ziglar. She completely embraced personal development and goal setting techniques helping her to realize her BIG goal of working for Zig Ziglar in 1994. Since that time, Michelle has journeyed through the ups and downs of life all the while holding on to her passion of inspiring, motivating and encouraging others to be the best that they can be.

Michelle has learned the secret to living a happier, more abundant life and she's on a mission to show you how to stop juggling, overcome procrastination and get more done in your business, leadership and life! It's time for "America's Productivity Coach" to give you the tools to STOP being busy being busy and start being a "Difference Maker."

Michelle Prince
CEO, Prince Performance Group & Performance Publishing
Best-Selling Author
Zig Ziglar Motivational Speaker
6841 Virginia Pkwy, Suite 103#124
McKinney, TX 75071
469-443-8768
Info@PrincePerformance.com

Faith, Family and Fortitude

By Keresa Richardson

I struggled with the idea that I should write a chapter for this book. I just didn't feel that my life was that extraordinary or that I have anything of value to share. I asked myself, "Why would anyone care what I have to say?" Then a dear friend pulled me aside (like only a good girlfriend will do!) She told me,

"You have a sphere of influence and you need to simply
give God the glory for what He has done in your life."

I thought to myself…"I can do that!" I am nothing, but God is everything. He is the Alpha & Omega, El Roi (The God Who Sees) and so much more! As women it's easy to diminish the impact that our lives have on those around us. We simply go through our daily responsibilities, take care of our families and focus on the tasks before us. But, can you imagine what life would be like without the influence of godly women in our families and in our world?

If you're reading this please realize that God has a divine purpose for your life. He loves you and you have great worth to Him. None of us are perfect but God is faithful and he molds our lives according to His plan. I truly believe that whatever I have accomplished or any good deed that I have ever done was God working through me.

Now the failures and mistakes in my life, I have to own those. I can't blame God for them but He forgives me and picks me up when I fail. And He puts me back on the right path over and over and over again! He is the perfect Father and I consider it a privilege to share my story of how He has worked in my life. I've highlighted a few key insights that I've learned along the way.

The Early Years - God has a sense of humor! I was born on Friday the 13th, met my husband on Friday the 13th and we married on the 13th. I consider every Friday the 13th my "Lucky Day"! I grew up in a Christian home and an entrepreneurial family. I was taught to work hard and play hard and God blessed me with strong role models who embodied perseverance. On the maternal side, my grandparents, Momma and Papa Stone, were nothing less than spiritual mentors to their children and grandchildren. They were farmers in the Red River Valley of Oklahoma. They worked very hard to provide a simple life for their children. Family time was always a high priority. Papa was a deacon in the small country church, and he was always the first person to arrive on Sunday mornings. After services, we loved going to Momma and Papa's farm where my mother was raised. Every Sunday after church we would have lunch as a family and the ten cousins would gather eggs, jump in the hay lofts and ride horses.

Later in life, Papa tenderly cared for Momma's every need as she suffered with Alzheimer's disease for seventeen years. Seeing such a faithful demonstration of God's love in a marriage left an indelible imprint on my heart. My mother followed her father's example and was every bit a spiritual giant in her petite 4'10" body! She has always been and still is my prayer warrior, support system and doting mother. From her I've learned compassion, and witnessed first-hand the joy that comes from unselfishly serving others.

Another early role model for me was my paternal grandmother. She was widowed during the Great Depression, and was left with a three year-old son. On his deathbed, my grandfather made the difficult decision to send for his in-laws and request that they raise his only son. He did this, because he knew that his wife would have to find a job and make her way in a man's world. The circumstances of life obligated my grandmother to go beyond her comfort zone. With the loss of her husband, she entered the workforce in order to send financial support to her son and her family. The professional experience she gained during the hard times of her life later served as a foundation for her own business endeavors. Eventually, she remarried, and opened her own antique shop.

Her life was never easy. But, this southern lady was able to weather life's storms and uses her personal experiences to influence others. She would later teach me how to properly set a table and the art of gracious entertaining. Her appreciation for the finer things of life and the sacrifices necessary to procure them spoke volumes to me. My father, having been raised in the absence of his parents, came to understand the importance of being self-sufficient. He was and still is a serial entrepreneur. The drive and ambition of a self-employed father and the love and tenderness of my spiritually-minded mother are obvious foundational elements in my life. On both sides of my family my relatives were extremely generous. Many times, despite their limited resources they provided food

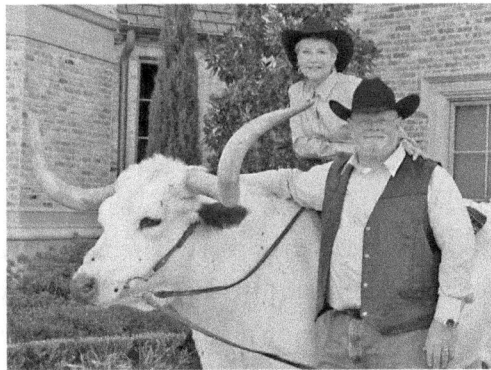
Keresa & JR Richardson on "Stickers" the longhorn.

and shelter for others in need. Demonstrating the love of Christ to whomever they encountered.

Insight: Spend as much time as possible with your children in their formative years. Instill in them a moral compass. It will enable them to make good decisions in life.

Even as a child my administrative gifts were evident…My first grade teacher told my mother that I would grow up some day to be president. In high school I was never the pretty cheerleader or the rich socialite but I could organize people and get things done. I was voted "Best Leader" and ran many of the school clubs and organizations. Always the overachiever, I put myself through college working one to three jobs simultaneously and still graduated in 3 ½ years.

I married just after college when all my friends were marrying. I was too young and didn't really understand what it takes for a successful marriage. Five years later, I was divorced and devastated—my huge failure. The one good thing from a bad marriage was my baby girl…life's richest blessing. She kept me going as my world fell apart.

Insight: God can bless you even in the midst of your failures. This too shall pass! Stay the course and keep your eye on Him.

Second Chances - God is a God of second chances. He never forgets or abandons us. We may move away from Him but he never moves away from us. He was just waiting for me to rely on Him and grow up, then he delivered to me my Soul Mate. At a family BBQ I saw a tall, blonde-haired, blue-eyed Texas man wearing jeans, a white shirt and a cowboy hat! (Hubba, hubba!) It was love at first sight! He later told me, as I walked away that day, he thought to himself, "There goes my next wife." It took a little longer for me. After our first date (the next day), I found myself humming the tune of "I'm getting married in the morning". (I think the Holy Spirit was working!) I married for love and not money. Twenty nine years later, we're still in love. Our love has grown and so has the money! But when you start with nothing the only direction to go is up.

Insight: The only things of true value in this world are: Love, Joy, & Peace. They are invisible, you can't see them and you can't earn them. You don't appreciate them until they are gone. I am so grateful for second chances!

A Blended family - Our lives were not easy- My husband had two boys from his first marriage and I had one daughter. We had total custody of all three children, so from day one of our marriage we had three children 24/7. (Yikes!) I was twenty-nine when we married and my two step-sons were twelve and fourteen years old. They were not happy about the new rules and routines in our home. They were accustomed to a "bachelor pad" with no living room furniture and only a pool table. No regular meal times, just frozen pizza. Now, we had dinner together as a family, there were curfews and we went to church!

I wish I had time to tell you the stories about blue jeans dried in the microwave and the cat tumbling in the clothes dryer. There was also the time our son cut a hole in the top of his car (Because he wanted a sun roof!) Many times I questioned if I or the children would survive…But God is faithful! And remember, He has a sense of humor! By the way, all the children are still living and the cat was fine. But the microwave…not so much.

Insight: Children need structure and boundaries. Pick your battles and don't squabble over the small stuff. (You can buy a new microwave).

"Tough Times Don't Last, Tough People Do" - The first ten years we were married we struggled financially. I worked in our business one day a week, home schooled our daughter, and was wife and mother. It was stressful but we were happy. After our daughter graduated from high school at sixteen my teaching career was over. My husband asked what I was going to do next. I had not given any thought to what I wanted. I was just busy trying to fulfill the necessary needs of the family. My first reaction to his question was to say "I plan to do NOTHING!!!! But, my entrepreneurial husband encouraged me to start another business. He said, "You have three college degrees and too much talent to do nothing." The idea of starting a new business struck a chord with me. Yeah! Why not? I think my grandmother would approve. We researched many options and decided to open a Benjamin Franklin Plumbing franchise. Now 13 years later, our business is part of a national franchise and I am currently serving my fourth year as brand president. It has been fun to help create a national brand. We have worked with some amazing people and learned so much.

Insight: You are never too old to start something new. God's timing is always perfect. Have faith in your God given talents and don't let your fears hold you back.

As our entrepreneurial journey has continued we have started other businesses and diversified into other industries. We have worked together day and night and the Lord has blessed our efforts. We now have the ability to share our blessings with others and do mission work in other parts of the world. We enjoy working in other countries and making a difference in the lives of children.

Insight: God can do anything, you know—far more than you could ever imagine or guess or request in your wildest dreams! He does it not by pushing us around but by working within us, his Spirit deeply and gently within us. *Ephesians 3:20* (The Message Translation)

Along with success comes a certain amount of criticism. On more than one occasion, I've been surprised that people judge my family and me harshly and assume that we are arrogant and proud. I call it reverse discrimination. We are all God's children and wealth is fleeting. Money and possessions can be gone in the blink of an eye. True joy comes from being content regardless of the circumstances.

If you're reading this and you are struggling…I want to encourage you that God can change your life. The moral to my story is that God can restore the years you have lost and he can turn rags to riches. (*Joel 2:25*) Just know that even if he doesn't he is still God. I have been rich and poor, fat and thin, abused and spoiled, happy and devastated, cherished and cast aside but I have never been alone. "The LORD himself will lead you and be with you. He will not fail you or abandon you, so do not lose courage or be afraid." *Deuteronomy 31:8* (The Good News Translation) ⚞⚟

KERESA RICHARDSON

You don't find too many women in the plumbing industry. But, Keresa Richardson, president of Benjamin Franklin Plumbing, believes that this trade definitely needed "a woman's touch". Keresa and her husband (J.R.) own several companies, some specializing in the mechanical trades. In 2013, they celebrated the 30th anniversary of their first business endeavor.

Keresa is passionate about women in business and works tirelessly to market her own companies in the competitive Austin, Dallas, Houston and San Antonio markets. Keresa believes in the power of quality service, customer satisfaction and the Golden Rule. She is a native Texan, a graduate of Texas A&M University, and holds two master's degrees.

The Richardson's were among the first "Pioneers" of the now nationwide franchise, Benjamin Franklin Plumbing and Keresa has continued to faithfully support franchisees nationwide as the Brand President for the past four years.

She funds mission work in South America along with many local charities. She also spends much of her time consulting with small business owners, serving in her local church, and is active in various community and political organizations. She is the mother of three children, has five grandchildren and four "grand dogs".

Keresa may be contacted for business consulting and speaking engagements by email at Keresa.Richardson@ benfranklinplumbing.com

Keresa Richardson
Benjamin Franklin Plumbing
1500 S. Central Expressway #300
McKinney, TX 75070
469.742.2301
Keresa@1LMC.com
www.Punctualplumberdallas.com

Go Do

By Wendy Shelley

I always felt as if I were being called to "go do" something in my life. It was like I was meant for something more, something bigger and something selfless. But I believed that you had to go to some distant land or far-away place to "go do." I wasn't willing to make that journey as a wife and mom. In addition, I didn't know what I would "do" if I did. I struggled with this feeling until a strange course of events came out of nowhere a little more than 12 years ago. My husband Steve wasn't looking for a job, but an offer came his way. As we prayed for decision-making and clarity, things fell into place. We trusted that this major move was being guided by a divine hand.

Now I realize that God was giving me an opportunity to grow where I was planted, to make a difference in my own community and to encourage others to do the same. It's a role that I've embraced, and now I love to share the message that we each can "go do" in our hometown, whether it's where we grew up or where we were transplanted.

Steve accepted the job offer with Volvo right after Christmas of 2000 and started almost immediately. He moved into a corporate apartment in Texas, leaving me in Michigan to get our house ready to sell in the dead of winter with Wyatt, who was seven months old, and Jordin, who was five. Our plan was to join him in late March. It ended up being one of the worst winters that the Detroit area had seen in years. I cursed having to shovel the snow, keep my house "show ready" with two small children, and then bundle them up and take them out on a moment's notice—only to have the real estate agent not show. We had only one low-ball offer in several months, and I was at the end of my rope. What were we thinking???

Although our house had not sold, I moved anyway. I arrived in McKinney, Texas, in late March. I was completely miserable and depressed. I'd left my family and friends—and still had a house nearly 1,200 miles away to worry about selling. I was in a foreign land; after all, I was a Yankee! To top it off, Wyatt, who was now 10 months old, decided to start crawling the day we arrived in our small corporate apartment. I now had something added to my list of anxieties. I didn't know where anything was, didn't have my support network, and Steve was traveling a lot. I would search the Bible, looking for verses about peace and contentment. Several months later, we learned that the Volvo regional office was closing and Steve would lose his job. Why did everything fall into place when we prayed over the decision to move here when it now appeared to be a huge mistake? It was all necessary for me to "go do."

Kim

In early April, the moving van arrived in McKinney and boxes began filling our new home. My neighbor, Kim Altizer, knocked on the door. She offered a plate of oatmeal scotch cookies and lots of invaluable advice. "Do go to this hospital, don't go to that one; be sure you get Wyatt on the waiting list for Crossing Point preschool—(he's not even a one-year-old yet, I was thinking, but she ended up right on that one!). Texas is a very buggy place, you'll need an exterminator. I have an excellent dentist…" She was, and continues to be, a Godsend in my life! Little did I know she would play such an important role in my "go do."

In the fall, Kim asked if I was interested in attending a *Bible* study. I thought, "Me? *Bible* studies were for those with vast knowledge of the *Bible*, who could spout off verses, and thump you over the head with them." I'm sorry, that had been my experience. Don't get me wrong. I've attended church my whole life, but never saw myself as a *Bible* study-*Bible* thumper. Yet I decided to try it, thinking, "Kim has been a Christ-like example to me since I moved in, and she's not beating me with a *Bible*."

We started Disciple 1 together that fall at Stonebridge United Methodist Church (11 years later, much of that original group still meets on Monday mornings at 9:30!). We read and studied the entire *Bible* in about nine months. The study concluded with a weekend retreat where we all discovered and discussed our spiritual gifts. I was told that I had administrative skills, compassion, the desire to serve and the ability to bring people together. I had never before thought about the gifts with which God had blessed me. I decided then that I had to take action—and "go do"—to use my gifts to glorify Him and serve my community. Thank you, Kim!

Jennifer and SRLA/MLA

I started by working on some projects at church, including the auction committee and teaching Sunday school (I was never very good at that!), but was still looking for more to "go do." When we first moved to Texas and Steve worked at Volvo, the company had donated a car lease to the annual fashion show auction organized by the Stonebridge Ranch Ladies Association (SRLA), now the McKinney Ladies Association (MLA). Dr. Jennifer Buchanan, a McKinney orthodontist, was SRLA president at the time. Steve was Volvo's contact person for the car lease, so we went to Eldorado Country Club to drop it off on the night of the auction. Jennifer found out that we had just moved to McKinney, I had left my network back in Michigan, and was home with two small children. She called me over the next several months with kind persistence, inviting me to the women's group meetings. I made excuses until finally I thought, "I am stuck here in Texas now and I can continue to be miserable or I can get out of the house." So, off I went. The women were welcoming and kind, and the next thing I knew, I was involved in planning their next fashion show.

Since participating in that first fashion show, I have chaired several of them. I recently completed my eighth year on the board—seven as president and one as past-president. As president of the organization, I helped open SRLA/MLA to all women in the area (not just those in Stonebridge Ranch) and we were twice honored as Hope's Door Volunteer Organization of the Year and recognized as Volunteer McKinney's Organization of the Year. We have supported, and continue to support, organizations such as Meals on Wheels, Community Lifeline Center, SPCA, CASA, The Food Pantry, Samaritan Inn, Seniors Helping Seniors McKinney, Mane Gait, and others,

McKinney Ladies Association (MLA) President, presenting scholarships to daughters of McKinney first responders.

with not only financial contributions, but also with volunteers, increased awareness and physical donations of much-needed supplies. My last act on the board was the approval of a $50,000 commitment during the next 10 years to the McKinney Public Safety Children's Scholarship Foundation. It has been amazing to watch this organization grow and flourish and such a blessing to see how the women of SRLA/MLA have positively impacted the community over the last eight years. I could not be more proud! Thank you, Jennifer, for persuading me to attend that SRLA/MLA meeting years ago and thus giving me the push to serve God more and "go do."

Serving Our Veterans

My connection with Jennifer doesn't stop there. Dr. Jennifer Buchanan is an amazing woman. Not only is she smart, beautiful and an incredibly savvy businesswoman, but she is passionate about helping others. Several years ago, Smiles Charity was born and a group of 10 or so volunteers (mostly women who stayed at home with their children) began producing a free family festival/concert event for the community. The popular event raises money to build a home for a family in need. In May 2013, Smiles Charity produced its sixth event and raised more money than ever to build a home for a war-wounded veteran and his family. The tears of joy from this young man and his wife as they were presented with the keys to their home were worth every minute of the year's worth of preparation that goes into the event. It is an honor to "go do" for our veterans, as they have given up so much for us.

Politics, and Thanks to Kim Again!

As an American, I feel it is vital to be a part of the election process—because much has been sacrificed to give us the right in this country to vote. Not long after I moved here, Kim invited me to a coffee event for a man running for the McKinney City Council in my district. Again, in an effort to connect and meet people, I agreed to go. I would have laughed then if you'd have told me that I'd actually be running this candidate's winning campaign in 2013 for his second term as McKinney's mayor!

When I met Brian Loughmiller at that coffee, I realized that I recognized him. I'd seen him and his wife Donna involved in church activities, volunteering at school, coaching teams and stacking chairs. I thought,

"Hmmm, this is someone I can get behind. He's not just 'talking the talk, he's walking the walk,' as the saying goes." Brian went on to defeat the incumbent and then completed a second term as City Councilman before making a run for the mayoral seat in 2009. I was honored when he and Donna approached me at church about being a part of his core campaign committee. It was an amazing group of people they put together, and everyone was up to the task. There were events to plan, signs to place, calls to make, forums to attend, and, ultimately, votes to get! I was tasked with keeping Brian's calendar, planning events, and making sure he got from point A to point B when needed. It was a tremendous amount of work, but we celebrated his victory on a rainy night that May.

In the fall of 2010, McKinney Councilman Ray Ricchi approached me about running his re-election campaign. I had gotten to know Ray well since our paths crossed frequently with school functions and a variety of community projects in which we both participated each year. We hit the ground running with a media blitz and appearances everywhere. Our strategy was to scare off the competition early on, and it worked. Ray ran unopposed, and in June 2011, was sworn in once again as District 4 councilman.

In 2013, Mayor Loughmiller drew an opponent just one hour before the filing deadline. This time, he asked me to be his campaign manager. We ran a fast and furious campaign, having mere months to prepare for the election compared to 2009 when we worked for the better part of a year. We were diligent, efficient and worked hard, and on Election Day in May 2013, we celebrated Mayor Loughmiller's re-election to another four-year term as the leader of our city.

Participating in these campaigns has been such a tremendous honor. I'm so proud to have represented people of such character and integrity, traits that are so rare in politics today. I am thankful to have met so many wonderful people from our city through my involvement in these campaigns. I have been blessed to be able to "go do" once again, this time as part the political process in our city, where important decisions are being made about the future of our community by leaders I admire.

Today, my "go do" projects include my new position as treasurer of the McKinney Boyd High School Bailadoras Drill Team. My daughter Jordin is a Bailadoras dancer. I am also honored to serve on The Heard Museum's special projects advisory board, Smiles Charity, the McKinney Public Safety Children's Scholarship Foundation Board of Directors, and provide my continued support to Stonebridge United Methodist Church. Of course, you will always find me at MLA events—I cannot give that up! Beyond, that, I'm not sure what the future holds, but I try to remain open to what God directs me to "go do."

I am so thankful for the gifts that God has revealed to me during the last 12 years. My hope each day is to glorify Him in all that I "go do," even if it's putting up fliers for an event, emceeing a program or standing out in the heat collecting entrance fees at the semiannual MLA yard sales. I am also thankful to those who have cultivated my gifts and challenged me to use them. I am especially thankful to Steve, Jordin and Wyatt for allowing me to "go do." I truly believe that without "going and doing," I would have withered away. "Doing" brings me such tremendous joy. My wish is that we all discover our gifts and find something we can "go do" that will not only bring us joy, but that will also give someone else joy. Now, let's "go do!"

WENDY SHELLEY

Wendy Shelley was born and raised in Clarkston, Michigan, and attended Michigan State University, where she earned a bachelor's of science in Merchandising Marketing. She spent her "career years" in the auto racing world, having worked in marketing and promotions for IndyCar. She currently resides in McKinney, Texas, with husband Steve, daughter Jordin and son Wyatt. She now considers herself a "professional volunteer." She is best known around McKinney for her role as president of the McKinney Ladies Association, but is also recognized for running successful election campaigns, most recently for the mayor. You will find Wendy in the McKinney City Council chambers, attending ground-breakings, at school board meetings, soliciting auction items, and backstage each May at the Smiles Charity Concert. Her tireless efforts to do good for her community are commendable, and McKinney is a better place because of them.

Wendy Shelley
Mom and Community Volunteer
214-695-6352
wendshel@aol.com

The Samaritan Inn

By Lynne Sipiora

I moved to McKinney fifteen years ago, kicking and screaming.

It was a job transfer for my husband and I was not enthusiastic. At the time, I was a stay at home mom to my three young children and a long time volunteer, following a career in not for profit management.

As a frequent mover, I knew that the best way to know in a community was to get engaged, so just as soon as the last moving box was unpacked I signed up at the Samaritan Inn.

The Samaritan Inn is Collin County's only homeless shelter. At the time, they housed fifty men and women, providing basic necessities and a program that led to independence.

Collin County has a variety of worthy not for profit organizations but I chose the Samaritan Inn because it seemed to me that no one can better their life until they know they have to food to eat and a place to lay their head at night.

Just as my youngest child was preparing to enter junior high, the board asked me to take the position of Executive Director. By coincidence (or perhaps fate), my first week on the job was the same week the Katrina evacuees came to Collin County. It was "baptism by fire".

People regularly ask me how I can bear all the sad stories. I certainly have heard my share, but the sorrow is always trumped by the successes.

Every day the Samaritan Inn takes in broken people in severe crisis and gives them the support, tools and encouragement they need to become independent. It is an honor to be just a small part of that transformation.

Hugh and Kenny were the first residents that I met. They had arrived at the Samaritan Inn on the very last bus that left ravaged New Orleans in 2005. Hugh wanted to finish his college degree and Kenny wanted to help people, in return for the help he had received. Two years after their arrival, Kenny was working at the Samaritan Inn telling our residents: "If I can do it, so can you", and I had the privilege of handing Hugh his degree as he graduated from Collin College.

Wilma arrived at the Samaritan Inn at age 85. She had been evicted from her apartment because her son had stolen all of her money. Wilma did not need to find work, like most of our residents, but she did need shelter and counseling. Wilma "mothered" the other residents and slowly got back her emotional strength. When her social security and pension were finally sorted out by our caseworkers, she moved to a senior living apartment, where she remains today. Wilma has Thanksgiving dinner with me every year and always says that she is thankful for her time at the Samaritan Inn. Imagine being thankful for living in a homeless shelter—but it was the turning point for Wilma, as it is for so many.

Single mom, Debbie, and her daughter, Erin, sat in their front lawn, amidst all of their belongings and cried when they were evicted from their home. Debbie had lost her job, quickly used all of her savings and could not pay her rent. A neighbor drove them to the Samaritan Inn. Today, Debbie has a great job at a local hospital and Erin is a National Merit scholar.

Toby, a single Dad, and his two teenagers lived in their car for 11 weeks as they waited for an opening at the Samaritan Inn. Toby wanted his son to have his senior year at McKinney High and was determined to get into the Inn and make that happen. Finally; in mid-October of the school year, there was an opening. Toby's son graduated number 11 in his class and received a full scholarship to the University of Texas.

None of these people fit the stereotype of the homeless guy, living under a bridge and holding a sign that reads: *Will work for food*. They are all people that had been contributing members of society until something happened. Sometimes homelessness occurs as a result of poor choices, but more often then not it is long term unemployment that begins the downward spiral. When you are in crisis, it is hard to develop a plan for the future. It is difficult to navigate the system in order to receive the services that you need and it's often impossible to independently pull yourself out of the depression and loss of self esteem that you feel.

My role at the Samaritan Inn is to be an advocate for the marginalized and speak for them when they are unable to speak for themselves.

My advocacy started early. I vividly recall riding the school bus with my little brother. He was six and I was eight. It was winter time and somebody grabbed my brother's hat and started throwing it from kid to kid, around the bus. My brother was humiliated, crying and paralyzed. I knew that this was unjust. I also knew that my brother was hurt and I knew somebody had to do something and it occurred to me that somebody was going to have to be me.

I told the bus driver he had to pull over and he had to get my brother's hat. Furthermore, I told him that he might want to say something to all the little brats that were involved. And he did just that.

It sounds melodramatic I know, but that is truly the exact moment that I realized I could make a difference. I could play a part in helping someone, who for whatever reason was unable at that moment, to help themself.

The Samaritan Inn has quadrupled in size over the last eight years. We have added a thrift store, an administrative building and an apartment complex for supportive independent living. Our shelter can now accommodate 160 people, but the need is still great. Our next project is a family shelter, because families are the fastest growing number in the homeless population.

Janine and Barry, a married couple with four young children, told me that "parents are supposed to take care of their children, that's what you do and to think that we can't is devastating".

Janine and Barry stayed at the Samaritan Inn for almost a year. Their two older children were enrolled in elementary school, while the two younger one went to daycare. At the end of their time with us, Janine and Barry both had acquired full time employment, had completed a mandatory financial course that taught them how to budget and had just put a down payment on a small home. More importantly, they were proud of their accomplishments and confident of their future. They arrived in tears and left in triumph, a tribute to their tenacity and the program at the Samaritan Inn.

We are all connected in this world and I believe that we are obliged to take care of one another. Many people never get to see the results of their help, but I do, everyday and I never cease to be amazed by the power of philanthropy and the strength of the human spirit!

LYNNE SIPIORA

Lynne Sipiora was born in Philadelphia, gradu-ated from Northwestern University in Evan-ston, Illinois and moved to McKinney 15 years ago.

She is a published author ("In Search of Motherhood", Addison Wesley Publishing Com-pany) and a frequent contributor to the Dallas Morning News. Lynne has thirty years of not-for-profit management experience and is cur-rently (2005 to the present) the Executive Director of the Samaritan Inn, Collin County's only homeless shelter. She is the recipient of the Ebby Halliday Rose of Distinction award, as well as the "Best Executive Director" award from the Texas Homeless Network. Lynne and her husband Ken live in McKinney and have three children—Ken Jr. 25, Daniel 21 and Maggie, 20.

Lynne Sipiora
Executive Director
The Samaritan Inn
www.the samritaninn.org

A New Beginning

By Maylee Thomas-Fuller

*T*here is no doubt in my mind and heart that this journey through life is orchestrated by a power much higher and greater than our own. We choose to believe that our day can be divinely ordered and we often experience the unexpected. Most of our relationships are indeed a direct manifestation of those divine orchestrations. This story is one of the most significant of these. It's a story of redemption and faith, rescue and hope, and in the end, simply about the sheer guts to step off a cliff into an unknown abyss with only a belief that" it's just the right thing to do". To recognize a connection beyond the physical realm…When you know in your "knower" that God has this and you're just along for the ride. We hope this blesses you in a way to be confident that the Lord is still working miracles today. We just need to learn to recognize them.

The Mission

I've been blessed to be a part of many "mission" trips while young due to my involvement in music. I traveled throughout college to many foreign countries with a group called Maranatha Repertoire Company.

Maranatha brought song and drama depicting the story of Jesus to places that had never heard the Gospel before. Later in my Christian walk, I was given the opportunity to bring aid and relief to remote parts of Mexico. Each trip was life changing for me and continued to seal my desire to do more for the less fortunate. My husband, however, had never been on an organized mission trip. Don't get me wrong, helping others has always been his way of life, but he had never experienced the power of an organized group effort. So, when the opportunity presented itself for him to go on a "Raiders of the Lost Ark" expedition with well-known Biblical Scholar and Archeologist, Bob Cornuke of Base Ministries, without hesitation, I said, "Go!" I had heard of Bob from the Discovery Channel documentaries about his search for Noah's Ark. I knew that this trip was going to change Geo's (my endearing nickname for my hubby George) life. I just didn't realize it was going to change our whole family's life.

It was a snowy January night in 2007 when sleet and icy roads had made our load-in for a gig that evening. Geo was carrying his guitar rig across the icy pavement when he stepped off the curb and his foot rolled over with the sound of 'crack'. His ankle swelled to the size of a grapefruit. I got a call from him, as I was en route to the performance. "Maylee, I think I may have broken my ankle. You may have to do this gig without me tonight". My heart sank. Honestly, I was upset about his injury, but even more perplexed about the timing of it. He was supposed to leave just nine hours later for his mission trip to Africa. By the time I got there, he was sitting in a chair with his foot elevated and the band crew surrounding him. "Can you stand on it?" we asked. "Do you think it's broken?" "Can you play guitar?" We all fired questions at him that he couldn't yet answer. I could see the stress on his face. "I think I just need to go to the emergency room." Well, then I knew that it was serious. My husband doesn't usually visit any doctor and especially visit the emergency room.

Okay, let me back up a bit…I must admit to my doubts approaching his date of departure. Just two weeks before, Egypt and Sudan were put on the hot list and warnings of terrorist attacks were buzzing in the media. Since their itinerary included Egypt and neighboring Ethiopia, I was concerned. I displayed some fear by suggesting that Geo wait to go on a later trip. When this happened to his ankle, I tried to make it a sign for him to stay. Thankfully, Geo didn't see it that way. He saw it as the enemy trying to keep him from going. He went to the emergency room for a proper diagnosis. When he found out that it was torn ligaments, he asked the doctor, "If I walk on my ankle will it cause any more harm?" "No", the doctor replied, "but you won't be able to really walk on it for a while." He didn't know the tenacity of my hubby! Geo replied, "Just give me a walking boot please; I have a plane to catch". So he came out with a big, black, bulky walking boot and pain meds, although I knew that he wouldn't take them. I couldn't imagine what the next few days held for him as far as pain, especially on a trip where there was A LOT of walking planned.

The Awakening

Three days passed. It was either in the middle of night, or early in the morning that I would get phone calls from Geo because of the time difference. Remember, it was an archeological trip, and they had scheduled stops in different remote areas to visit monks and sites that were believed to have been along the journey that the Arc had taken. Its final resting place was believed to be Axum, Ethiopia. The residents of Axum claim that the Arc is securely guarded under the Church of Zion, located in the center of town. Bob Cornuke had sifted through years of artifacts and made many trips back and forth to document his findings in order to gain the trust of the Ethiopian people. He was now given an opportunity to share his findings with those on the expedition.

The group trekked through miles of terrain. However, Geo wasn't going to let his mishap slow down the rest of the group. Instead, he forged on. Unfortunately, by the end of each day, Geo would be in so much pain that he could not sleep. As the third day came to a close, Bob and the group doctor became very concerned about Geo's health. He had literally gone without any sleep since arriving in Ethiopia. The doctor decided to administer a shot with a "sleep cocktail" that was often used in the field during surgeries. When Geo called me that third night to let me know what was about to transpire, I knew that he was REALLY suffering. I've seen him literally run around a doctor's office, trying to avoid a shot (to be fair, that time it was a very big needle!). When Geo called me at 11:00 PM (his time) to let me know that the doctor had arrived and that he would be "out" a minimum of eight hours, I was grateful that he would finally get some much needed rest. And it worked, well, the "rest" part. Geo woke up refreshed and rested for the first time on his trip. He looked at his watch and it was 12:30 in the morning. He called. "I can't believe it," he told me on the phone, "I slept through the night and the whole next day"! He was completely rested but disappointed to have missed out on a full day of travel. Can you imagine his surprise when I told him that we had talked just over an hour ago, not 25 hours ago! "How can this be?" he asked, "I feel fantastic, wide awake and ready to go," he said. He told me he was going to walk the streets of the city and he would talk to me the next day.

Geo sadly noticed many children sleeping on the streets that night. The children were very young and rolled up trying to stay warm. They were all over the square of the small remote town. Geo wondered why there were so many children who were not in homes. Later, at breakfast, the doctor was shocked to see Geo awake. Geo told him what had happened. The doctor said it was all but impossible for Geo to have awoken less than an hour after being given the shot and had he not administered it himself, he wouldn't have believed it. Then Geo asked Bob about the children on the streets. "Most are from the local orphanage", Bob said. "They don't have enough beds for all the children so at night, when they close the gates and the children without a bed try to find shelter at local churches until the orphanage re-opens in the morning." He added, "Those that don't find shelter in the churches, have to fend for themselves outside". Geo wanted to go to the orphanage and survey the situation. Bob tried to dissuade him, explaining that St. Yared, an almost forgotten orphanage, would be too difficult a situation for him to see. Geo, feeling like this may have been God's purpose for him to be on the trip, insisted that he go. The group was on a tight schedule and deviating from it would set things behind. However, the group bought into Geo's "feeling" of his purpose and agreed to make the stop. After all, he had risen from a completely "dead" sleep to witness what he had; there must have been a Divine Influence!

One in a Million

My husband is a prolific writer. Although we co-write songs together and often collaborate on lyrics, I know that he has a gift that is way beyond mine for words. In fact, for special occasions I always tell him that I prefer a love letter to anything else. I keep them around my house in out-of-the-way places so I can refer to them for encouragement and inspiration. I asked him to recount the day's event for you.

In Geo's words, "As I entered the rusty gates of St. Yared Orphanage, I felt a tremendous sense of despair and hopelessness. I was told by Bob Cornuke, the Biblical Archeologist I was traveling with, that this place was not visited by Westerners and no children had ever been adopted out of St. Yared. In a culture that strongly believes that an AIDS infected male could cleanse his body by having sex with a virgin, young children lived at risk as they entered adolescence. St. Yared, I learned, had beds for 75 children which meant that the balance of the 331 orphans who gathered there during the day would have to find shelter elsewhere every night. There was no running water or electricity and the one meal a day was prepared in a makeshift, rusted out metal panel hut over an open fire on the outside dirt floor. I was overwhelmed to say the least.

I knew at that moment that my purpose on the trip to this land was to be at St. Yared. I was not sure what we could accomplish but I knew we had to do something. Therefore, I began to survey the compound. As I moved about there were many small children who gathered at my side. All of them were clamoring to hold my hands, singing a simple song with the chorus "My God is good". I knew that God was good, but I was amazed how they saw that through their very underprivileged and sunken, nutrition starved eyes. Nonetheless, these little children smiled, laughed and sang. That is, all but one. I noticed at my arrival a very thin, older little girl that seemed to watch me with a sense of fear, or certainly caution. Although she followed me from point to point, she did so from twenty feet away, biting her nails and crouched over in a defensive like posture. I felt that I needed to approach her and put her mind at ease about my presence. However, I was worried that she would flee.

At one point, Bob came over to me and began to share his concern about these children. It is at that time that Bob educated me about the culture, the AIDS danger and the desperate plight of these children. Bob concluded our conversation with a rhetorical question; "do you know the chances of these children making it to adulthood?" With an almost involuntary reflex, I responded with "One in a million"? Man, I was disgusted with my response. Where did that come from? It was a rhetorical question and didn't require a response...definitely not a trite one! I don't use that expression and certainly that was not a response that was commensurate with the levity and depth of the content that Bob had just shared with me. I was embarrassed by my words and walked off. In my path was the little girl, still biting her nails. She watched me intently as I approached her, and to my surprise, stayed to greet me. I called over the young interpreter that was traveling with us and asked him to ask her name. As he spoke with her, I replayed the exchange that I had just had with Bob in my head. "One in a million, how could I make such a trite remark", I asked myself.

At that moment, the little girl responded with her name…"Million" she uttered. I could not wrap my head around what she had just said…I asked him to ask her again…. "Million" she replied with an angelic smile. That moment is when I felt that God put his hand on my shoulder."

The Phone Call

It was Saturday morning in downtown Denver, Colorado. I hadn't heard from Geo since his midnight stroll when he had only slept for an hour. He asked me if I could talk. At that moment I could tell he had something significant to say. The room went silent. Had they found the Arc? How awesome that would be. For thousands of years they had been looking for it. It would be such an incredible discovery. Millions of people would now be able to see that the Bible is not just a book of stories, but an actual account of history. This must be the life changing experience that I felt Geo would have to share. I wasn't prepared for what he had to say next. "Honey" he said, "I know that you aren't here to experience what I am, but I know that if you were, you'd feel the same way that I do. I've been visiting an orphanage all morning with horrific conditions. These children have no running water or electricity, no bathrooms, and most of the beds are without mattresses or blankets. Most of the children are without shoes and only have the clothing on their backs. They look as if they haven't eaten for days. The next sentence silenced the room that I was in. All of the clatter of utensils that I had been listening to for the past thirty minutes was gone. I only heard Geo say, "And honey, I think we are supposed to adopt a little girl here"

Milyan and George

The day we met Milyan

105

What did he just say? Adopt a little girl? This was the man, who at the birth of our third child said, "no more!" You could have knocked me over with a feather. He kept saying, "Honey, you aren't here to see and experience this with me…but I believe we are supposed to adopt a child".

Upon Geo's return, we did make the decision to adopt our precious daughter, Milyan, and the process of adoption and bringing her to the United States was a story all in itself, full of anticipation and emotions, not to mention heartache after we realized that we couldn't yet bring her home.

We fled to St. Yared Orphanage in Axum, Ethiopia just weeks after his return so that I could meet Mily and share in the bond that Geo had started with her. I wondered if she would be as welcoming to me. It played out like an orchestrated movie when he called to her and she fell into my arms with both of us weeping. And in Geo's humor he said "What about me? I'm the one that found you"! We all laughed, and later in the week, realized that Mily had a great sense of humor, just like her "Dad". We had brought her a shirt with our family picture on it. Ruby had superimposed her picture with us so it would be "complete." Above the picture it read "Our Family." We wanted her to have it to keep while she waited through the process of adoption, to remind her that we were coming back for her. Geo would go through each face and say, "Mommy, Layla, Raine, Austin, Mily and, when he pointed to himself, he'd say Handsome". After days of this, she finally asked someone what handsome meant. She just laughed about it, but would shake her head "no" to him when he would call himself Handsome. When it was time for her to go to the new facility with one of our translators, we all hugged and cried uncontrollably. We kept telling the interpreter, please tell her we will be back to get her and bring her home. We promised. But, I wondered if she really thought that would happen. In the midst of all that sorrow, Mily, with tears rolling down her face, took her little finger and pointed to Geo's chest and said, "Handsome." Daddy lost it.

There was no way we weren't going to come back for our daughter, whom in only days we had bonded with on an emotional and spiritual level that you would only understand if you experienced it. This was a divine intervention, and what God started, I knew He would finish. Boy, did I ever have to trust that in the process. Reminding ourselves that God would open the doors that needed to be opened, after so many had been shut in our face, literally. He did finish, just hours before our flight was to leave that sweltering hot August day. She was officially ours. And in anticipation, she knew very few English words, but would ask me every stop home (and there were many on the 38-hour trip), "AMERICA "? Her brilliant green eyes lit up when I finally answered, "Yes, baby, America".

As we walked through the front door, there were about 35 to 40 smiling faces to greet our new addition to the family. Many had helped tirelessly with donations for the orphanage and they were all lined up in a circle to each give her a flower. To our surprise, Mily (our nickname for Milyan) would give them each a hug as she circled the room. She was very shy at the beginning, but as we have learned, that was only until she felt comfortable, because this child is certainly not shy. There were tears flowing as Milyan would hug each person and in her timid little voice say "thank you".

7 years after we met, Milyan's Sweet 16

Looking back at that day, one of my favorite moments was when we took a group picture in front of the fireplace and she was right in the middle of us all. No super imposed face was needed. My recollection is most clearly God's presence when everyone was gone and we just huddled up on the love seat in the foyer and tried to communicate with her about what she thought of the day.

It was very special seeing her face light up as she looked around the room and we told her "this is your home now."

Remarkably, this journey began because Geo felt a desire to go to Africa in January. It was now August 10, 2007, which was in the eighth month of that year. I had learned many years before that number eight, in Biblical meaning, is *new beginning*. It was indeed a new beginning. For all of us. ☞

MAYLEE THOMAS-FULLER

My family.

Maylee Thomas-Fuller is best known in Texas as the soulful lead singer of the Maylee Thomas Band, where she performs regionally in clubs as well as festivals and concert events with her husband and guitar player, builder and developer George Fuller. She and her husband co-founded the Love Life Foundation in 1992, a non-profit organization created to bring awareness, aid and refuge to women and children "at risk". Maylee and George reside in McKinney, Texas where they have four children, Austin, Raine, Layla and Milyan. They own the Guitar Sanctuary music store and Performance Academy in McKinney as well as the Sanctuary Music and Event Center, in the beautiful Croatia inspired village of Adriatica.

Love Life Foundation
6633 Virginia Parkway
McKinney, TX 75070
http://www.maylee.com/
www.facebook.com/mayleethomas
http://www.lovelifefoundation.com/
http://www.theguitarsanctuary.com/

www.ingramcontent.com/pod-product-compliance
Lightning Source LLC
Chambersburg PA
CBHW070835100426
42813CB00003B/620